SLEEP

C000001327

by Matilda Feyiṣayọ Ibini

‖ SAMUEL FRENCH ‖

FOR AMATEUR PRODUCTION ENQUIRIES

UNITED KINGDOM AND WORLD
EXCLUDING NORTH AMERICA
licensing@concordtheatricals.co.uk
020-7054-7298

Each title is subject to availability from Concord Theatricals,
depending upon country of performance.

SLEEPOVA was first produced at the Bush Theatre in London, England on 24 February 2023. The cast was as follows:

FUNMI (OLUWAFUNMILAYO) .... Bukky Bakray
REY (ALFREDA).................................... Amber Grappy
SHAN (SHANICE)................................. Aliyah Odoffin
ELLE (GABRIELLE) .... Shayde Sinclair

The role of Funmi's Dad was voiced by Jude Akuwudike

The creative team was as follows:

DIRECTOR .... Jade Lewis
SET & COSTUME DESIGN .... Cara Evans
LIGHTING DESIGN .... Elliot Griggs
SOUND DESIGN .... XANA
COMPOSER.................................. Romarna Campbell
MOVEMENT DIRECTOR .... Gabrielle Nimo
COSTUME SUPERVISOR......................... Imogen Brown
VOICE & DIALECT COACH .... Gurkiran Kaur
FIGHT & INTIMACY DIRECTOR .... Enric Ortuño
PRODUCTION DRAMATHERAPIST................. Wabriya King
DRAMATURGY............................... Deirdre O'Halloran
CASTING DIRECTOR .... Jatinder Chera
ASSISTANT DIRECTOR (PLACEMENT) .... Apoorva Anagalli
PRODUCTION MANAGER .... Pete Rickards for eStage
COMPANY STAGE MANAGER .... Lucy Ventham
ASSISTANT STAGE MANAGER................... Sophie Haliburn
PRODUCTION TECHNICIAN....................... Rori Endersby
REHEARSAL SCRIBE............................. Jennifer Okolo

CAST & CREATIVE TEAM

BUKKY BAKRAY | Funmi (Oluwafunmilayo)

Bukky began her acting career in the breakout indie hit *Rocks*, directed by Sarah Gavron, in 2020. The film won Bukky several awards, including the prestigious BAFTA Rising Star. Bukky starred in the BBC/Netflix series *You Don't Know Me*, starring Sam Adewunmi, which received positive critical acclaim. She will next be seen in *The Strays*, a Netflix UK original film opposite Ashley Madekwe, and Apple TV+ series *Liaison*, alongside a cast including Vincent Cassell and Eva Green. Her other credits include short films Gospel *According to Gail* and *Self Charm* directed by Ella Greenwood.

In 2020 she was selected for the BAFTA Breakthrough programme and included in the annual Dazed 100 list. Bukky was named as one of the Screen International's Stars of Tomorrow 2021.

AMBER GRAPPY | Rey (Alfreda)

Amber trained at LAMDA and spent a large part of her third year working first on HBO's *The Baby*, playing one of three lead women. She was recently seen in the BBC show *Wreck*, a slasher-comedy which will return for a second series in 2023. Amber is currently filming *One Day* for Netflix, and *Sleepova* marks her professional stage debut.

ALIYAH ODOFFIN | Shan (Shanice)

Upon graduating from RADA in 2021, Aliyah was quickly snapped up by Working Title to play one of the leads in *Everything I Know About Love*, which landed her a Royal Television Society North West nomination in 2022. Her theatre debut in Clybourne Park garnered her fantastic reviews, and most recently she led the cast alongside Alfie Allen in *Suffrajitsu*, a short film produced by Steve McQueen's production company, Lammas Park.

SHAYDE SINCLAIR | Elle (Gabrielle)

Shayde is presently training at the Guildhall School of Music and Drama and makes her professional stage debut in *Sleepova*. Her voice credits include *Phantoms*, *Visions* and *Siren Voices* (part of a BBC Radio 3 Series).

MATILDA FEYIŞAYỌ IBINI | Writer

Matilda Feyişayọ Ibini (she/they) is an award-winning, bionic playwright and screenwriter of Nigerian heritage from London. Matilda was awarded a scholarship from BAFTA and Warner Bros to study a Masters in Playwriting & Screenwriting. Matilda was selected as a Star of Tomorrow 2020 by *Screen Daily Magazine*, a feature film screenplay they co-wrote with Gabriel-Bisset Smith was selected as part of The Brit List 2020 and they were an Arts Foundation Futures Award 2021 Finalist.

As a playwright, Matilda has had residencies with Sphinx Theatre, English Touring Theatre, Soho Theatre, BBC Writersroom, Graeae Theatre, and the National Theatre Studio. Matilda's debut play *Muscovado* was produced by BurntOut Theatre, premiered in October 2014 and subsequently co-won the Alfred Fagon Audience Award. Their audio drama *The Grape that Rolled Under the Fridge* was broadcast on BBC Radio 3. Matilda's next play, *Little Miss Burden,* was produced by Harts Theatre Company and the Bunker Theatre; it premiered at the Bunker Theatre in 2019, was a finalist for an OffWestEnd Award for Best New Play, won a Popcorn Finalist Award 2020 and was published by Concord Theatricals.

Screen credits include: BAFTA TV-nominated *CripTales* for BBC America and BBC4; *Unprecedented* series, Headlong & Century Films for BBC4; *Head Over Wheels*, a short film produced by Open Sky Theatre and Wrapt Films which won two awards at the 2021 Digital Culture Network Awards; and *MO <3 KYRA*, a short film produced by Film4 and 104 Films.

Matilda's work has been staged at the Old Vic Theatre, Shakespeare's Globe, Royal Court Theatre, Bush Theatre, Soho Theatre, Arcola Theatre, Bunker Theatre, Hampstead Theatre Downstairs, Royal Exchange Manchester, Hackney Showroom and Vaults Festival.

Matilda has screen projects in development with BBC Films, Home Team, Ardimages UK and Raw TV.

JADE LEWIS | Director

Director Jade Lewis was a Boris Karloff Trainee Assistant Director at the Young Vic, a Creative Associate at the Gate Theatre and held an International Residency in Thailand in 2018. Jade most recently wrote and directed *Get Dressed!* at the Unicorn Theatre, a short film for the TWENTY TWENTY project with the Young Vic, *Quarter Life Crisis* at the Bridge Theatre, co-created an original audio series *World Of Curls* with the writer Yolanda Mercy for BBC Radio 4, and directed an audio drama *NSA* which was a part of Talawa Tales also BBC Radio 4. Jade is the Carne Literary Associate at Theatre503.

CARA EVANS | Set & Costume Designer

Cara Evans (she/they) graduated from the RCSSD with first class honours in 2019. Cara is an associate director at OPIA Collective and a reader at the Royal Court.

Theatre includes, as Designer or Co-Designer: *The Living Newspaper* (Royal Court); *Sirens* (Mercury Colchester Studio); *Get Dressed!* (Unicorn); *Queer Upstairs* (Royal Court); SK Shlomo: *Breathe* (Royal Albert Hall); *Bright Half Life* (King's Head); *Blanket Ban* (New Diorama/Underbelly); *Ordinary Miracle* (NYT Studio); *Instructions for a Teenage Armageddon* (Southwark); *The Woman Who Turned Into A Tree/Refuge* (New Nordics Festival/Jackson's Lane); *The Girl with Glitter in her Eye* (Bunker); as Associate Designer for Chloe Lamford: *Teenage Dick* (Donmar School's Tour).

ELLIOT GRIGGS | Lighting Designer

Elliot Griggs trained at RADA.

Theatre credits for the Bush: *The P Word*; *Hir*.

Theatre work includes: *Amélie the Musical* (Criterion/Other Palace/ Watermill/UK Tour. Nominated for Olivier Award for Best New Musical); *Fleabag* (Wyndham's/SoHo Playhouse, New York/Soho Theatre/Edinburgh Festival/Tour. Nominated for Olivier Award for Best Entertainment or Comedy Play); *Jitney* (Old Vic/Leeds Playhouse/ Headlong); *Purple Snowflakes and Titty Wanks*, *A Fight Against*, *On Bear Ridge* (Royal Court); *O, Island, Ivy Tiller: Vicar's Daughter, Squirrel Killer* (RSC); *The Wild Duck* (Almeida); *The Lover/The Collection* (Harold Pinter); *An Octoroon* (Orange Tree/National); *Missing Julie* (Theatre Clwyd); *Ivan and the Dogs* (Young Vic); *The Trial of Josie K* (Unicorn); *Richard III* (Headlong); *Disco Pigs* (Trafalgar Studios/Irish Rep, NY); *Dry Powder* (Hampstead); *Pomona* (Orange Tree/Royal Exchange/National. Off West End Award for Best Lighting Designer); *Queens of the Coal Age*, *The Night Watch* (Royal Exchange); *Feeling Afraid As If Something Terrible Is Going To Happen* (Roundabout. Fringe First Award); *Missing People* (Leeds Playhouse/Kani Public Arts, Japan); *Yen* (Royal Court/Royal Exchange); *Psychodrama* (Traverse); *Blue Door* (Ustinov Studio); *Loot* (Park/Watermill); *Somnium* (Sadlers Wells); *The Misfortune of the English*, *Last Easter*, *The Sugar Syndrome*, *Low Level Panic*, *Sheppey*, *buckets* (Orange Tree); *Lampedusa* (HighTide); *The Oracles* (Punchdrunk); *Martha, Josie and the Chinese Elvis*, *Educating Rita* (Hull Truck); *Shift*, *Bromance* (Barely Methodical Troupe).

Event and Exhibition Design includes: 100 Story Hotel (Discover Story Centre); Lost Lagoon, Height of Winter, The Single-Opticon, Alcoholic Architecture (Bompas & Parr).

XANA | Sound Designer

Xana is a freestyle live loop musician, sound artist, vibrational sound designer, archival audio producer, audio researcher, spatial audio installation artist and theatremaker. Xana also develops accessible sound systems for spaces, is a sound arts facilitator and is a music tech lead at music research and development label Inventing Waves.

Theatre credits for the Bush: *The P Word*; *Strange Fruit*.

Theatre: *Everyday* (Definitely Theatre, New Diorama); *Who Killed My Father* (Tron Theatre); *The Trials*, *Marys Seacole* (Donmar Warehouse); *...cake* (Theatre Peckham); *Sundown Kiki, Changing Destiny, Fairview, Ivan and the Dogs* (Young Vic); *as british as a watermelon* (Contact Theatre); *Burgerz* (Hackney Showroom).

ROMARNA CAMPBELL | Composer

Romarna Campbell's storytelling begins with the drums. The nomadic spirit of this exciting drummer, producer and composer lives in her jazz and hip-hop-infused music. Her irrepressible energy can be heard on *Inherently Political*, a super-charged sonic assault on racism that immediately won favour with Anne Frankenstein, Jazz FM's Tony Minvielle and had her crowned by Jamz Supernova as New Name of the Week.

Her independently-released kaleidoscopic debut, *25 Songs For My 25th Birthday*, features Soweto Kinch, Tomeka Reid, Sumi Tonooka and Lady Sanity and takes us deeper into her world of resonant frequencies and conscious vibrations.

Having honed her craft with Berklee College of Music, Tomorrow's Warriors and the Notebenders, Romarna stands on the shoulders of giants and is drawing inspiration from the view as she beats a path forward that is very much her own.

GABRIELLE NIMO | Movement Director

Gabrielle Nimo has worked with Talawa Theatre Company and Emergency Exit Arts on Creating Routes, a training programme for facilitators. Since then she has taken on a number of roles, including Dance Captain for *Everything That Rises Must Dance* (Complicité), Movement Director for Nouveau Riche's *TIMBUKTU* (Gerry's Cafe, Theatre Royal Stratford East), Director of Harrow Arts Centre Youth Theatre and most recently, Movement Director for *Unknown Rivers* (Hampstead).

Alongside her work in theatre, Gaby currently teaches Movement at Foundation, BA (Hons) and MA Level in Drama Schools.

DEIRDRE O'HALLORAN | Dramaturg

Deirdre O'Halloran is the Literary Manager at the Bush Theatre, working to identify and build relationships with new writers, commission new work and guide plays to the stage.

At the Bush, she's dramaturged plays including Olivier Award-winner *Baby Reindeer* by Richard Gadd, *Lava* by Benedict Lombe and *An Adventure* by Vinay Patel.

Deirdre was previously Literary Associate at Soho Theatre, where she worked as a dramaturg on plays including *Girls* by Theresa Ikoko and *Fury* by Phoebe Eclair-Powell. She led on Soho Theatre's Writers' Lab programme and the biennial Verity Bargate Award.

As a freelancer, Deirdre has also been a reader for Out of Joint, Sonia Friedman Productions and Papatango.

GURKIRAN KAUR | Voice & Dialect Coach

Gurkiran Kaur is a voice, accent and dialect coach from London. She received her BA in Drama and Theatre Studies from Royal Holloway, University of London before training as an actor at The Bridge Theatre Training Company. She has an MA in Voice Studies from The Royal Central School of Speech and Drama and is part of Freelancers Make Theatre Work's Dawn Chorus collective. Gurkiran works at a number of drama schools and with private and corporate clients. She is part of The Voice and Speech Teaching Associations' EduCore Leadership Team and serves as a Junior Board Member.

Theatre credits for the Bush: *Paradise Now!*; *The P Word*; *Favour*; *Red Pitch*.

Other coaching credits include: *Extinct* (Stratford East); *Queens of Sheba* (Soho); *NW Trilogy* (Kiln); *How to Save the Planet When You're a Young Carer and Broke* (Boundless Theatre); *Best of Enemies* and *Chasing Hares* (Young Vic / Headlong); *Lotus Beauty* (Hampstead / Tamasha); *Henry VIII* (Globe); *Offside* (Futures Theatre); *Marvin's Binoculars* (Unicorn); *The Climbers* (Theatre by the Lake); *Finding Home* (Curve); and *Good Karma Hospital* for Tiger Aspect Productions.

ENRIC ORTUÑO | Fight & Intimacy Director

Enric Ortuño is a Spanish Fight and Intimacy Director based in the UK. He is a certified Stage Combat teacher by the British Academy of Stage and Screen Combat, a certified Intimacy Director by Intimacy Directors and Coordinators USA and holds an MA in Movement Studies from the Royal Central School of Speech and Drama.

He is a resident teacher at Italia Conti Acting School and regularly teaches at RADA, Central School of Speech and Drama and Drama

Studio London, and has taught workshops in Spain, the USA, Canada and Germany.

Fight and Intimacy credits for theatre include the National Theatre of Scotland, National Youth Theatre, National Theatre Connections, Nottingham Playhouse, Orange Tree Theatre, King's Head Theatre, Arcola Theatre, Ovalhouse, Trafalgar Studios, and Theatre 503 amongst others.

Intimacy Coordination credits include productions for and by Warner Bros, Apple TV, BBC, Netflix, Channel 4, Amazon Studios and Sky TV.

WABRIYA KING | Production Dramatherapist

Wabriya King's practice is to create a space and a format to hold people safely while they navigate their experiences in relation to the theatre's work. Wabriya has previously worked on productions at Soho Theatre, Theatre Royal Stratford East, Hampstead Theatre, Royal Court, National Theatre and Paines Plough.

Credits for the Bush include: *Paradise Now!*; *The P Word*; *House of Ife*; *Red Pitch*; *Overflow*; *Lava*; *The High Table*.

IMOGEN BROWN | Costume Supervisor

Since graduating from The Royal Central School of Speech and Drama in 2020, Imogen Brown has specialised in costume designing/supervising and wardrobe management for theatre and film.

Her past projects include Costume Designer/Supervisor for the feature film *Venice at Dawn*, dressing for *Birmingham Royal Ballet*, working with the Royal Court as Costume Assistant and the National Youth Theatre, Mountview and the Actor's Touring Company as Costume Supervisor. In 2021, she also worked as a fashion assistant for designer Harris Reed on multiple projects, including their debut collection For Now, Unexplained, Olly Alexander for The Brits 2021 and Iman for the 2021 Met Gala. Most recently, she worked as Wardrobe Assistant and Lead Dresser for the Birmingham 2022 Commonwealth Games.

JATINDER CHERA | Casting Director

Jatinder Chera took a position at the Royal National Theatre, following his graduation from the Casting Certificate, at the National Film and Television School. Prior to this, he worked as an actor, having trained at Millennium Performing Arts.

For the Bush, Jatinder cast: *The P Word* (dir. Anthony Simpson-Pike). Further credits include: *The Nutcracker* (Bristol Old Vic, dir. Lee Lyford); *Up Next Gala 2022* (Lyttelton Theatre, choreography Stephen Mear); and *A Family Business* (Staatstheater Mainz & UK Tour, dir. Lekan Lawal).

As Casting Associate, he worked on: *The Father and the Assassin* (Olivier Theatre, dir. Indhu Rubasingham).

As Casting Assistant, Jatinder worked on: *Othello* (Lyttelton Theatre, dir. Clint Dyer), *Much Ado About Nothing* (Lyttelton Theatre, dir. Simon Godwin); *Small Island* (Olivier Theatre, dir. Rufus Norris); *Trouble in Mind* (Dorfman Theatre, dir. Nancy Medina).

APOORVA ANAGALLI | Assistant Director (Placement)

Apoorva Anagalli is a theatre practitioner from India specialising in theatre direction and acting. Currently, she is pursuing M.A. Theatre Making at the University of Kent, Canterbury. She is a recipient of the prestigious Charles Wallace India Trust Scholarship. She received her theatre training at the famed National School of Drama in India. Along with theatre she is also trained in Indian classical dance form Bharatanatyam and Carnatic classical music. She has experience of directing ten plays in Indian (Hindi and Kannada) languages.

PETE RICKARDS FOR ESTAGE | Production Manager

Pete is an experienced production manager and technical consultant within the performing arts industries. He has undertaken numerous technical and design roles across multiple disciplines alongside production management, meaning he is well placed to understand the complexity of roles within the production team.

Pete has managed shows throughout the UK and Europe for over a decade at venues including The Roundhouse, Hackney Empire, Schaubühne (Berlin), Birmingham Repertory Theatre, Soho Theatre, Liverpool Everyman, Battersea Arts Centre, Midlands Arts Centre, Birmingham O2 Academy, and Nottingham Playhouse.

Pete has also designed, built and run immersive experiences for clients, including Merlin Entertainment and The Tussauds Group.

He has toured and worked with musicians and artists worldwide for many years, including: Frank Carter & The Rattlesnakes, Shit Theatre, B Team, Sikth, We Are the Ocean and Mallory Knox.

Theatre credits for the Bush include: *House of Ife*.

LUCY VENTHAM | Company Stage Manager

Lucy Ventham is a London-based stage manager who frequently works on new writing.

Her most recent credits include: the world premiere of *On The Ropes* (Park/The Production Exchange); the nationwide tour of *Reasons You Should(n't) Love Me* (Paines Plough); the South West outdoor tour of *Estella* (Theatre6); *Mohand and Peter* (PYSCHEdelight / Southwark Playhouse).

She has worked for various off-West End venues, including Southwark Playhouse, Park Theatre and Kiln Theatre.

SOPHIE HALIBURN | Assistant Stage Manager

Sophie Haliburn trained at Rose Bruford College in Stage Management.

As Assistant Stage Manager: *Reasons You Should(n't) Love Me, Wife of Willesden, NW Trilogy, The Invisible Hand* (Kiln Theatre); *Bridgerton* (Secret Cinema).

As Props Assistant: *Billy Elliot* (Leicester Curve); *Madhouse* (Ambassadors); *Oklahoma* (Young Vic); *Translations, Ocean at the End of the Lane, Mr. Gum and the Dancing Bear – The Musical!, If Not Now When?, Anna, Downstate* (National Theatre); *Orpheus and Eurydice, The Mask of Orpheus* (London Coliseum); *A Taste of Honey* (National Theatre tour).

Bush Theatre 50
EST. 1972

We make theatre for London. Now.

Celebrating its 50th Birthday in 2022, the Bush is a world-famous home for new plays and an internationally renowned champion of playwrights. We discover, nurture and produce the best new writers from the widest range of backgrounds from our home in a distinctive corner of west London.

The Bush has won over 100 awards and developed an enviable reputation for touring its acclaimed productions nationally and internationally.

We are excited by exceptional new voices, stories and perspectives – particularly those with contemporary bite which reflect the vibrancy of British culture now.

Located in the newly renovated old library on Uxbridge Road in the heart of Shepherd's Bush, the theatre houses two performance spaces, a rehearsal room and the lively Library Café & Bar.

bushtheatre.co.uk

Bush Theatre

Bush Theatre, 7 Uxbridge Road, London W12 8LJ
Box Office: 020 8743 5050 | Administration: 020 8743 3584
Email: info@bushtheatre.co.uk | bushtheatre.co.uk

THANK YOU

The Bush Theatre would like to thank all its supporters whose valuable contributions have helped us to create a platform for our future and to promote the highest quality new writing, develop the next generation of creative talent, lead innovative community engagement work and champion diversity.

MAJOR DONORS
Gianni & Michael Alen-Buckley
Charles Holloway
Georgia Oetker
Tim & Cathy Score
Susie Simkins
Andrew Stebbings
Jack Thorne

LONE STARS
Jax and Julian Bull
Clyde Cooper
Jim & Michelle Gibson
Charles Holloway
Anthony & Mariela Marraccino
Georgia Oetker
Susie Simkins

HANDFUL OF STARS
Charlie Bigham
Judy Bollinger
Catharine Browne
Sue Fletcher
Priscilla John
Simon & Katherine Johnson
Garry Lawrence
Robert Ledger & Sally Moulsdale
Vivienne Lukey
Aditya Mittal
Bhagat Sharma
Dame Emma Thompson

RISING STARS
David Brooks
Philip Cameron & Richard Smith
Penelope Christie
Lauren Clancy
Tim Clark
Richard & Sarah Clarke
Susan Cuff
Matthew Cushen
Ivo Detelinov
Jubilee Easo
Emily Fletcher
Jack Gordon
Hugh & Sarah Grootenhuis
Thea Guest
Sarah Harrison
Uzma Hasan
Lesley Hill & Russ Shaw
Melanie Johnson
Ann Joseph
Davina & Malcolm Judelson
Joanna Kennedy
Mike Lewis
Lynette Linton
Michael McCoy
Judy Mellor
Caro Millington
Kate Pakenham
Sophie & Tom Pakenham
Raj & Kim Parkash
Mark & Anne Paterson
Stephen Pidcock
Karen & John Seal
Oliver Stocken
Peter Tausig
Joe Tinston & Amelia Knott
Jan Topham

CORPORATE SPONSORS
Biznography
Harper Collins
Nick Hern Books
S&P Global
The Agency
Wychwood Media

TRUSTS AND FOUNDATIONS
29th May 1961 Charitable Trust
Backstage Trust
Buffini Chao Foundation
Daisy Trust
The D'Oyly Carte Charitable Trust
Esmée Fairbairn Foundation
Garrick Charitable Trust
Hammersmith United Charities
The Harold Hyam Wingate Foundation
John Lyon's Charity
Kirsten Scott Memorial Trust
Martin Bowley Charitable Trust
Orange Tree Trust
Teale Trust

And all the donors who wish to remain anonymous.

If you are interested in finding out how to be involved, please visit **bushtheatre.co.uk/support-us** email **development@bushtheatre.co.uk** or call **020 8743 3584**.

CHARACTERS

FUNMI (Oluwafunmilayo) – she/her, black, starts play age fifteen, of Nigerian heritage.

REY (Alfreda) – she/her, femme, black or black-mixed race, proudly Queer, various ages, plus-size, starts play age fifteen, of Grenadian and English heritage.

SHAN (Shanice) – she/her, black, various ages, starts play age sixteen, of Nigerian and Jamaican heritage, has sickle cell.

ELLE (Gabrielle) – she/her, black or black-mixed race, various ages, starts play age fifteen, of Jamaican heritage.

AUTHOR'S NOTES

This is to black girls and femmes whose parents never allowed them to attend sleepovers – well consider this play an invitation. You are safe here. You can be yourself here. You can dream here.

This play encourages collaboration, for example the ethnicities described in the cast list are open for you to adapt to the performers playing a specific character. This also means there is some degree of flexibility in tweaking details or slang to fit specific cultures.

Some people might wonder – Matilda why's there so much swearing in this. Because young people swear, maybe not in front of you but they do. I wanted to write a play about a bunch of girls who resist respectability which is often forced and projected onto black girls. These are characters pushing back against having their language policed. Now I understand it may not be appropriate for school productions, that's when I encourage some imaginative thinking in swapping out the swearing but any other future professional staging of this play – I want to hear every syllable of every fucking word.

This is my second full-length play to be published. *Sleepova* is my third produced full-length play in a now twelve-plus-year career. (Take that imposter syndrome!)

Care, joy, direction and comfort is at the heart of this play, so ensure it's embedded in the production too!

....

A – at the end of a line of dialogue or stage direction means an interruption.

/ means two or more characters talking over each other. If at the start of a line of dialogue, it can also indicate when the next character should begin speaking over the other character.

... means a brief break, longer than a beat but shorter than a pause. Can also mean when a character struggles to form words in their mouth.

Suggested interval after Scene Four but only if needed.

The music mentioned in the script is suggestive rather than prescriptive.

Content Warnings

Strong language
Experiences of living with sickle cell
References to and description of mental illness and physical illness
Frequent themes of and references to homophobia, racism and sexism
Absent parents
Mention of a rape alarm
References to grief and bereavement

ACKNOWLEDGEMENTS

Infinite thanks to my family: Adebanke, Tolulope, Ayotunde, Babajide, my relatives and my ancestors. What an honour it is to love and be loved by you.

Huge thanks and love to everyone who read drafts at different stages, supported the production in some capacity and just generally supported me whilst writing:

Lynette Linton, Deirdre O'Halloran, Daniel Bailey, Sarah Zadie Baiden, Debbie Hannan, Oladipo Agboluaje, Jules Haworth, Nikki Disney, Ola Ince, Tito Oye aka @hersickledjourney (Instagram & TikTok), E.M Williams, Bola Akeju, Leanne Henlon, Jack Thorne, Phoebe Éclair-Powell, Jess Burgess, Judith Merry, Laura Merry, Jude Akuwudike, Abi Falase, Aleeyah Watson, Jordon Stevens, Sulaiman Khan, Gabriel Bisset-Smith, Jen Tan, Carol Ellis, Jess Thom, Matthew Pountney and everyone at Touretteshero, elop: LGBT Mental Health & Wellbeing charity. Soho Theatre's Writers group way back in 2011, when this idea first crystalized. Thank you to the team and volunteers at Revitalise Sandpipers for their support and kindness during my stay to crack open this play. And thank you to FlawBored for their guidance on physical self-descriptions.

Huge love and thanks to my tireless champion and agent Ikenna Obiekwe – here's to many more fruitful years and even greater heights with you.

To the phenomenal constellation of talent: Aliyah Odoffin, Amber Grappy, Bukky Bakray and Shayde Sinclair – I have so much love for all of you. What exciting careers you all have in store!

Massive thanks and huge love to the exceptional creative team behind the production: Oscar Owen, Jatinder Chera, Cara Evans, Imogen Brown, XANA, Pete Rickards, Lucy Ventham, Sophie Haliburn, Romarna Campbell, Gabrielle Nimo, Apoorva Anagalli, Jennifer Okolo, Nikita Karia, Gurkiran Kaur, Wabriya King, Elliot Griggs, Helen Murray and Doug Kerr (for the wicked poster!) – thank you all so much for your hard work, astronomical talents and unwavering belief in the story. Thank you to the team at Concord for publishing my second full-length play and for their continued support of my work!

Big ups to Jade Lewis – director extraordinaire and all-round legend! Your support, enthusiasm and wisdom has meant so much to me. Thank you for bringing your heart to this production and going on this whirlwind of a journey with me.

My super and dedicated team of PAs (past and present): Mona, Alex, Emilie, Vanessa, Tarmin, Jaida, Lujayna, Inga, Rebecca and Hadiza (thank you for the late nights, pep talks, typing duties, and patience).

Sleepova is a blueprint of collective dreaming and would not exist without an empathetic community of dreamers.

To all the Black girls, women, femmes, non-binary peopledem of the past, present and future who continue to find ways to stand firm and upright in a crooked world.

PRESHOW

(The **CAST** *introduces themselves to the audience. They each provide a physical self-description; this is a type of audio description where a performer vocalises their own visual appearance. Physical self-descriptions should not be about identity, no one is being asked to out themself in any way or make the performer uncomfortable, but rather it is done to address a physical access issue and helps to level the playing field so this show is as accessible to as many people as possible.)*

(Self-description details can include: your real name and the character/s you will be playing, ethnicity, hair colour and hair style, height and any noticeable details like glasses, braces, piercings etc.)

(The **CAST** *tosses a 'theatre etiquette' ball to each other, saying their least favourite audience behaviour rules.)*

CAST 1. No honest reactions!

CAST 2. No fidgeting!

CAST 4. No snacking!

CAST 3. No getting involved!

CAST 2. No getting up to go toilet!

CAST 4. No getting comfortable!

(One of them pierces the ball with an object of their choosing. They watch it deflate. They all stomp on it together, toss in some wrestling moves.)

ALL. *(Variously.)* YEAHHHH! / Die! Die! Die! / Oloshi! And if I see you round these ends again yeah –

CAST 1. Sorry – theatre etiquette is not welcome here!

CAST 2. We want every kind of body to feel welcome in this space.

CAST 3. Cough till your lungs collapse.

CAST 4. Okay maybe not that. Just don't stifle it.

CAST 1. You don't have to wait till there's a loud bit in the story.

CAST 3. Same goes with farts, we want you to feel comfortable.

CAST 1. Not that comfortable. However –

CAST 4. – Should you need a break, feel free to leave and then return. There'll be someone to assist you back to your seat.

CAST 1. Turn your phones off or put them on silent. The play isn't even that long – *kay*.

CAST 2. Can we all do that now quickly, phone check, crep check, fine check. Yeah, you're all looking damn good today.

CAST 1. Especially you. I see you.

*(All the **CAST** blow a kiss or wink at someone in the audience.)*

CAST 3. Cos I swear if we hear a phone go off, this is the look you'll get.

(They all give their best mean, vicious death stare to each direction of the audience.)

Taking me out of character *bumbaclart*!

CAST 4. And if you miss a bit –

CAST 1. – Just grab a copy of that super accurate play text, that was published before we even opened.

CAST 2. We are not new to this.

CAST 3. We're true to this. *(Crosses fingers.)* Promise.

CAST 4. Who here's ever been to a sleepova?

CAST 1. Raise your hand, clap, nod, woop, wink, wave.

> *(The* **CAST** *encourages the audience to raise their hands or whoop. The* **CAST** *can ad-lib here.)*

CAST 2. Well this is for anyone who wasn't ever allowed to go to a sleepova.

CAST 4. Or wasn't invited to a sleepova.

CAST 1. Or whose mum picked her up at half eleven – before eye crust could even form like little canary diamonds in her eyes.

CAST 3. It's okay friend – heal.

CAST 4. Well you have now.

CAST 2. Cos you're officially invited to ours.

CAST 3. We're popping your sleepova cherry.

CAST 4. Don't worry we'll be gentle.

CAST 3. I've got protection.

> *(***CAST 3*** whips out a bottle of hand sanitizer, they use some and share it with the rest of the* **CAST.***)*
>
> *(Once they are all sanitized, they each put on their bonnet, silk head scarf or durag. They*

high-five each other and gass each other up,
like a team before a big match.)

(The **CAST** *exits to get ready.)*

Scene One

(Shan's bedroom. September 2016.)

*(**SHAN** is cleaning her bedroom. She carefully takes down her anime posters but leaves her Paramore poster up. She hides the posters somewhere discreet in her room. She chucks her cuddly toys into the bottom of her wardrobe and throws clothes on top of them for good measure. She runs up and down her bedroom with Impulse body spray, she starts to cough. She smells herself and sprays some over her clothes and then sprays some more around the room. She empties a bag of popcorn into a bowl.)*

*(**ELLE** knocks before she enters with a sleeping bag and a large backpack.)*

ELLE. Aloha! Smells like the girls' toilets here.

SHAN. It's not that bad, is it?

ELLE. Let's just open –

*(**ELLE** opens the door.)*

*(**SHAN** tries to disperse the smell with a pillow.)*

ELLE. I've got Haribo, Maoams, milk choc digestives – dark choc tastes evil, torch, first-aid kit, Swiss Army knife and brought my dad's laptop, it can play DVDs too –

SHAN. You are a literal lifesaver.

ELLE. Oh your present –

> (**ELLE** *rummages into her backpack and brings out a small, neatly-wrapped gift.*)

> (**SHAN** *snatches the gift from* **ELLE**'*s hands and excitedly tears it open. She looks at the gift peculiarly.*)

A keyring... necklace?

ELLE. It's a rape alarm.

SHAN. ...Thanks.

ELLE. Yours has this really cool laser on it. So you can blind rapists, murderers, serial killers, satanists – they usually hunt in pairs. And it'll give you enough time to escape.

> (**ELLE** *points the laser at the ceiling.*)

SHAN. I really appreciate all this Elle.

ELLE. *"Whoever is generous to the poor lends to the Lord, and he will repay him for his deed"* – proverbs 19.

SHAN. We're not – my mum has a morning and a night job, but she just doesn't get a lot of money.

ELLE. I know.

> (*Beat.*)

SHAN. We're going to have so much fun, our very first sleepova! I can't believe we convinced all our parents.

ELLE. My dad's picking me up at midnight.

SHAN. Elle – but you said –

ELLE. – Yes that I could come over but not that I could sleep over, my mum wasn't having it.

SHAN. Did you try –

ELLE. – I tried everything in the plan. I gave them your mum's number, her email, I even gave them your mum's work address. I told them your mum is a Christian and she goes to church every Sunday, she's not a tourist Christian. I even showed them the personal statement your mum wrote. It did work because I am here, but they will pick me up at midnight.

SHAN. Alright Cinderella, I knew I should have got my mum to do a DBS.

ELLE. My mum says why should I be sleeping in other people's houses when I'm not homeless.

SHAN. It's fine. You're here that's all that matters.

> (*The sound of a buzzer buzzing a little too excitedly.*)

I'll go let them in.

ELLE. Relax birthday girl, I'll get it.

> (**ELLE** *exits to answer the door.*)

REY. *(Offstage.)* Where's the birthday girl?

> (*Giggling can be heard from outside the bedroom.*)

> (*Shan's door swings open.* **REY** *and* **FUNMI** *come bursting in, rounding off the sleepova.*)

> (*The four of them excitedly do their not-so secret chant.*)

REY & FUNMI. ALOHA BITCHES!

ELLE & SHAN. ALOHA BITCHES!

REY. Konnichiwa cunts.

ALL. Konnichiwa cunts.

FUNMI. Sayonara later-loser.

ALL. Sayonara later-loser.

REY. O dabọ forever.

ALL. O dabọ forever.

> *(Their chant descends into giggles.)*
>
> *(**FUNMI** hugs **ELLE** then **SHAN**, but **REY** hugs **SHAN** and very briefly hugs **ELLE**.)*
>
> *(**FUNMI**, **REY** and **ELLE** freestyle a soulful version of* **[HAPPY BIRTHDAY]** *to **SHAN**.)*
>
> *(**REY** gets out a lighter and lights a cupcake.)*

(Sing) HAPPY BIRTHDAY TO YOU!
HAPPY BIRTHDAY TO YOU!
HAPPY BIRTHDAY DEAR SHAN!
HAPPY BIRTHDAY TOOOOOOOOO YOUUUUUUUUU!

FUNMI. Close your eyes and make a wish.

> *(**SHAN** closes her eyes, and blows out the candle.)*

SHAN. My wish has already come true.

> *(**REY** smears the cupcake in **SHAN**'s face.)*

Rey!

> *(**FUNMI** and **REY** laugh while **ELLE** helps **SHAN** to wipe her face.)*

REY. It was only a teeny cupcake.

SHAN. I wanted to eat that.

REY. Your present's better *(Winks.)* – promise.

> *(**REY** hands **SHAN** an envelope.)*

SHAN. Aww thank you Rey.

FUNMI. It's from both of us.

REY. It's not.

(**SHAN** *opens the envelope, it's a birthday card.*)

SHAN. Oh my days! A hundred-pound MAC voucher. Rey this is too much.

REY. I don't seem to hear a thank you.

SHAN. Thank you!

(**SHAN** *hugs* **REY**.)

REY. Got to make sure our girl's always looking flawless. We can't all wake up looking like me. I stole some posh seaweed face masks from my step-mum, they don't work on her saggy old skin but they should work for us. Don't know what my dad sees in that sea creature, when all they do is argue.

(**FUNMI** *and* **REY** *unpack their things.* **FUNMI** *takes off her jacket to reveal pyjamas.*)

Don't tell me you've been wearing that the whole time we travelled here?

FUNMI. I didn't want to waste any time changing.

REY. We sat on the bus. That same bum, you sat on the bus with, is the same one you want to be sharing a mattress with me.

SHAN. Ew, bus bum.

ELLE. It's not hygienic.

FUNMI. Whatever fam. Now open mine next. I hope you like it.

(**FUNMI** *hands* **SHAN** *an envelope.*)

(**SHAN** *opens the envelope.*)

SHAN. Happy Birthday Sailor Moon-Shan! Wait – what are these?

FUNMI. – So found out I can't officially donate blood until I'm seventeen, ageist bastards – like what's wrong with my blood? It's fresh, this is premium plasma they could be tapping into. So instead I convinced my dad and my sister to donate blood in my place. Didn't bother asking my mum, she'll think her blood could be used for rituals and she doesn't like the idea of accidentally saving her enemies.

ELLE. Rah, you got your family to give blood?

(**FUNMI** *nods proudly.*)

FUNMI. The way I see it, if I ever needed blood I'd want at least five pints from every single one of you that claims to love me.

ELLE. The human body only carries ten pints.

FUNMI. Just say you don't love me **joh**!

SHAN. You're actually the best.

FUNMI. My dad's already booked his next one.

REY. That's not a present... cheapskate.

(**SHAN** *hugs* **FUNMI**.)

FUNMI. Blood is priceless. More precious than any common voucher.

ELLE. It's true. Christ's crucifixion was an act of love. True Christians believe in transubstantiation. So giving blood is an act of love too.

FUNMI. *(Pause.)* See even our resident Pastor approves.

(**FUNMI** *high-fives* **ELLE**.)

REY. Well you still need make-up when you die so.

SHAN. I feel all funny inside.

ELLE. Good funny or bad funny?

SHAN. Definitely good. Like I feel really happy you're all here. Can we get a pic? Rey your phone's got the best camera.

*(They all get in close and pose with **REY***'s *phone camera.)*

REY. Fortunata fruits!

ALL. Fortunata fruits!

(The phone camera flashes.)

REY. Three... two... one.

(They all hiss/screech like vampires.)

You're an elder now Shan! Don't worry I'm coming to join you in ten months.

FUNMI. This time next year we'll be done with every last wretched demon –

REY. – At St Josephine Fortunata Girls.

ELLE. Finally!

FUNMI. Clap for yourselves – clap for yourselves.

(They all clap in celebration.)

ELLE. So how does it feel? Being legal now.

SHAN. Still got two more years Elle.

FUNMI. Nah it starts now – once you get your national insurance number. Means they can tax you now.

SHAN. Who's taxing me – when I don't have a job?

FUNMI. Her Majesty, the Queen – we pay all her bills.

ELLE. You can join the army too.

FUNMI. And you can do your theory test.

REY. Nah you can't take your theory till you're seventeen. Trust me I checked. I'm so done taking public transport.

FUNMI. You can take your theory at sixteen if you get disability. Don't you get disability benefits for your sickle cell?

SHAN. Nah, I don't qualify.

FUNMI. Oh my bad.

ELLE. You can get married now too but you still need a permission slip from your mum.

REY. Or a civil partnership?

FUNMI. You can have sex now, legally. The law looks at you like a big woman now.

REY. But you also don't have to have sex, because boys are gross and their bits look like something an alien vomited and put in a blender.

FUNMI. You're going to need to stop with all this cartoon **orisirisi jati-jati** Shan, its unbecoming of a woman.

SHAN. Woman! Nah I'm not in a hurry.

REY. You don't get to choose when you become a woman.

ELLE. The Lord has already made that choice for us.

FUNMI. Because really and truly –

REY & ELLE. – And truly and really –

FUNMI. – Mandem are not going to want to sniff you let alone touch you with all those cartoon posters on your wall.

SHAN. How did you –

FUNMI. – Think I can't see the blue tack marks everywhere. To you lot I'm Funmi, but to the world I'm Oluwafunmilayo Holmes bitch.

SHAN. I thought mandem were into cartoons.

FUNMI. Not the mandem that you want.

> (**SHAN** *nods, taking this in.*)

REY. Oh my God. Oh my God. How could I forget? You won't believe which wastegirl asked me to prom?

FUNMI. How many invites does that make?

REY. Five but who's counting? It's not my fault I'm every straight girl's dream.

FUNMI. *(Pushes back her lips.)* Gummy Grace?

> (**REY** *shakes her head.*)

SHAN. *(Shimmies her shoulders.)* Jiggly Jessica?

ELLE. Fiona?

> (**FUNMI**, **SHAN** *and* **REY** *look at* **ELLE**, *confused, in silence.*)

(Places whole hand on her forehead.) Five-head Fiona?

ALL. Ohhhhh.

REY. Rancid Rita.

> *(They all gag.)*

FUNMI. Hmmmmph.

ELLE. Why would she ask you?

FUNMI & REY. What's wrong with her/me?

ELLE. Nah I just meant she's not in your league... like that was brave of her.

FUNMI. So what did you say then?

REY. Obviously never in her dreams or nightmares. I told her that I'd only take her seriously if she cleaned under her fingernails, brushed her tongue properly and sorted out her acne.

FUNMI. Cold.

SHAN. One day someone is going to slap you for that mouth of yours.

REY. And I'll give it to them back.

> (**REY** *throws a fake slap back like she's playing tennis.*)

ELLE. You got your dresses for prom?

REY. Mine's a suit. My step-mum's paying for it. It's custom. Made her get me real gold cufflinks too, she's trying to bribe me to like her. I'm going to look sickening.

FUNMI. My dad took me to Roman Road market. We found this dress - it's buff man. Bejewelled corset then like a long flowy thing, think Brandy's Cinderella dress, but like better. He made sure I got everything I wanted – shoes, bag, jewellery.

ELLE. My mum's getting mine done at her tailor's, it's the same tailor that made her wedding dress, so I'm excited to see what she makes for me.

...Shan?

SHAN. My aunty's making mine.

ALL. *(Variously.)* Ohhh / That's nice.

SHAN. It's a skirt and blouse but, it'll look like a dress.

FUNMI. We're all going to look so fire.

> (**SHAN** *tries to change the subject.*)

SHAN. Yeah. Anyone you'd take to prom from the boys school?

ELLE. No. I don't know any of them.

REY. *(Snort-laughs.)* Cos you always have to go straight home after school.

SHAN. Don't worry your parents won't find out you had a thought about a boy.

I want to go with Jonah Asamoah in year eleven. I like how his first name rhymes with his surname.

REY. But he's so short, man. I couldn't like someone that only came up to my kneecaps.

SHAN. He's really cute. He has dimples, his afro's always neat and he has braces.

(**REY** *and* **FUNMI** *roll their eyes.*)

REY. Braces are the opposite of cute.

SHAN. When he smiles it actually sparkles, like he's wearing jewellery but on his teeth. And he always has the sickest creps. Like his laces glow in the dark.

REY. I'm not going with –

ALL. *(Variously.)* – We know. / You hate men. / You're allergic to boys.

REY. I never said that. I don't hate all men, I just very much dislike most of them – that's different. If we didn't go to an all-girls school then maybe I'd dislike them less. Have some respect for them but all I see are these beings that start licking their lips at the mere sight of a pleat on a school uniform. Like I am not allowed to exist without their approval, always wanting to make sure I remember my place... don't let boys run you like a dog. Hashtag feminism.

SHAN. *(Claps.)* Funmi, who would you go to prom with?

FUNMI. It's between two.

SHAN. *(Chuckles.)* Two?

FUNMI. Yeah Anthony and Antoine.

ELLE. Aren't they twins?

SHAN. As in identical twins?

FUNMI. It makes it so much harder. Anthony knows how to dress but Antoine's hair and breath are always on point.

REY. Have you ever actually spoken to them?

FUNMI. Yeah, when we had that fire evacuation and in McDonald's sometimes. But I never know which one I'm talking to...

ELLE. Um maybe we should all go together to prom? That way no one gets left out.

REY. Elle on feminist tings!

(**REY** *high-fives* **ELLE***!*)

We don't need dates to have fun!

ELLE. And I think I can convince my mum to let me stay out later if it's just us and no boys around!

FUNMI. Well it's not like anyone's asked us anyway. You in, Shan?

SHAN. Yeah...

REY. You should sound a little more enthusiastic Shan. Prom is to celebrate the end of our school's tyranny in our lives. We've been set free. So before we leave – we need to get mash up!

ELLE. Fortunata Feminist Tings!

(*Awkward silence from the others.*)

REY. So, bestie, what you got planned for us tonight then? Orgy, séance, astral projection?

SHAN. Sorry to disappoint but my mum did leave money for pizza, Elle brought her dad's laptop so we can watch films on that. Mum's just down the road at my aunty's, so she's giving us till one a.m.-ish then it's lights out when she comes back.

REY. You ain't got a laptop Shan?

SHAN. *(Nervous.)* No... not yet. I'm barely at home and they have TVs in hospital.

FUNMI. So is Solomon here to like watch over us?

ELLE. No it's a boy-free zone, just how it should be.

FUNMI. What if I drown?

REY. What?

FUNMI. He's a lifeguard. He knows CPR.

SHAN. Where Funmilayo? How?

FUNMI. I'll be so real. I don't feel safe without him here.

ELLE. Hands up if you've taken any first-aid training?

> *(**ELLE** is the only one to raise her hand.)*

Okay. As a trainee first-aider, I will carry out frequent risk assessments throughout the night. No one's prematurely dying on my watch. Funmi – I will keep you safe.

FUNMI. Let me die – **joh**! I don't want you... I want Solomon.

I'd be all over him like cocoa butter.

ELLE. I'd be all over him like Christ's love for mankind.

REY. Why do you always got to make it weird?

SHAN. Can we stop talking about my brother now?

FUNMI. One second.

> *(**FUNMI** lets out a moan.)*

Cool.

ELLE. Still can't believe your mum left us your whole yard.

SHAN. Just for a few hours though. I told her we are young ladies, and we are entitled to our privacy.

FUNMI. I could never say that to my mum.

REY. You played your sick card didn't you?

SHAN. ...It's the only card I've got.

ELLE. My mum gets worried if I'm in the bathroom too long.

REY. Probably thinks you're masturbating.

ELLE. No I am not. I don't even know what that is. Don't lie on my name like that.

REY. Okay, okay it was just a joke... but why did you get upset if you don't know what it is? How do you know masturbating isn't a hairstyle, or a swimming technique?

> (**ELLE** *gets flustered.*)

Not like you could find your salmon strips, under all that bush – sorry I mean burning bush.

> (**REY** *and* **FUNMI** *cackle.* **SHAN** *tries to stop herself from chuckling.*)

FUNMI. I imagine like you've got bush spirits, hunters and Babalawos.

REY. Yeah! She's got a whole ecosystem down there!

> (**ELLE** *doesn't look impressed.*)

SHAN. For someone who's failing Geography, surprised you know what an ecosystem is.

ALL. OOOOOOOOOHHHHHHHHHH!

FUNMI. She just called you dumb. Are you going to have that? Are you going to have that because I wouldn't have that.

REY. You know what, you can have that because it's your birthday.

FUNMI. So what we watching then?

SHAN. *The Hunger Games: Mockingjay*?

FUNMI. I didn't like how they did that little black girl dirty in the first film.

SHAN. *Twilight*?

REY. You mean your people?

>   (**SHAN** *sweetly gives* **REY** *the middle finger.*)

You know in that movie yeah when she comes in and Edward can smell her? Is she on her period?

SHAN. No! They're in love!

REY. I'm just saying, yeah, he's at this school, there's probably bare girls on their periods? What's so special about her period?

FUNMI. Stop talking about periods!

REY. I just like films with some accuracy!

FUNMI. It's not a documentary.

REY. Let's look on Putlocker, we'll defo find something on there.

ELLE. I don't feel comfortable doing this on my dad's laptop. He's gonna find out and then you'll never see me at any birthday ever again.

>   (**REY** *puts her hand on* **ELLE**'s *shoulder.*)

REY. Don't worry I'll erase the history.

ELLE. Are you sure?

REY. I've been erasing histories for so long; the government doesn't even know who I really am.

>   (**ELLE** *hesitantly lets* **REY** *on the laptop.*)

>   (**REY** *snatches the laptop and begins typing.*)

In Putlocker we trust. (*Hits a key on the laptop.*) Pick a genre.

(**SHAN** *and* **FUNMI** *hover over* **REY**.)

ELLE. No horrors please, or at least not too gory. I can't even watch *Casualty*.

FUNMI. *Suicide Squad*?

REY. I've already seen it, it's not scary enough.

SHAN. I haven't seen that new X-Men, that looks good.

REY. Hmmm... Or we could...? Nah forget it.

FUNMI. Nah, what?

REY. I know a film none of you have seen, and it's on here. It's about a mother struggling with her sick child, approaches this priest for special prayers and they invite him to come bless the sick girl. But I don't want to spoil it for you.

SHAN. I... does she die at the end?

REY. No. I wouldn't make us watch a film like that... it's uplifting.

FUNMI. What's it called?

REY. *The Exorcist*.

ELLE. I don't know about that.

REY. Elle this film has been used to train Priests, so it's basically been ordained.

ELLE. It's Shan's birthday, she should choose.

SHAN. Erm ...we can watch it.

ELLE. Shan, where's your school Bible?

SHAN. I'll get it for you.

ELLE. Okay. You don't happen to have any olive oil I could use?

FUNMI. You are not ordained to bless anything, girl sit down.

> (**SHAN** *goes to get her Bible and hands it to* **ELLE**. *She also grabs her rosary from where it's hanging on her wall.*)

SHAN. You can hold my rosary as well.

> (*They* **ALL** *gather round the laptop.*)

REY. This film is educational. It's about survival and how nothing in this life is ever as it seems.

> (*They open sweets and snacks and get comfortable as the film begins.*)

ELLE. ...I'm not sure I can watch this –

REY. It's literally just adverts. It hasn't even started yet.

ELLE. Yea, though I walk through the valley of the shadow of death,

I will fear no evil;

For You are with me –

> (*The electricity in* **SHAN**'s *room cuts out.*)

> (*They* **ALL** *scream.*)

REY. What the fuck?

FUNMI. Is there a blackout on the whole block?

ELLE. (*Looks out at the window.*) Nah neighbours' lights are still on.

REY. So your mum not pay the bill?

SHAN. We don't get bills like that – I'll go get the electricity key.

ELLE. No.

REY. Why?

ELLE. Divine intervention.

> (**ELLE** *gets her head torch out from her bag, puts it on her head and turns it on.*)

FUNMI. Why do you have that?

ELLE. It's important to be ready for any and all emergencies. Flood, fire, locusts, pestilence.

FUNMI. This is East London not Egypt.

> (*The sound of a car honking its horn outside.*)

ELLE. That'll be my dad.

SHAN. You're going already.

FUNMI. The night's barely begun.

ELLE. You know what my mum's like.

REY. Leave your head torch.

ELLE. O...kay.

REY. Thanks.

> (*REY hugs **ELLE**.*)

FUNMI. So unfair man.

> (*ELLE hugs **FUNMI**.*)

ELLE. Have fun and stay safe. Call 999 if anything happens then call me. Happy Birthday Shan. Sixteen looks good on you.

> (***SHAN** hugs **ELLE***)

ELLE. O dabo forever.

ALL. O dabo forever.

> (*ELLE exits.*)

Scene Two

(Funmi's bedroom. March 2017.)

(There's a bunk bed. A crucifix high upon the wall. A TV, a games console and two bean bags.)

(They all sit in silence watching the TV for a beat. **SHAN** *is still fatigued and recovering from a crisis but is trying to play it down in front of the others.)*

*(***FUNMI*** hands out revision notes. She hands out separate notes for each subject.)*

FUNMI. Shan - R.E, English and Geography.

SHAN. Ah, life-saver, thank you-thank you-thank you.

ELLE. Oh my gosh, what is that under the duvet?

FUNMI. It's a snake.

*(***ELLE*** covers her eyes.)*

REY. Maths please.

FUNMI. I got you fam.

REY. She cursed him, so any time he gets horny –

SHAN. – Shut up, man – I can't hear the subtitles!

(They all burst into laughter except **SHAN**.*)*

FUNMI'S DAD. *(Offstage.)* Ladies it doesn't sound like you're studying up there.

*(***FUNMI*** gets up and opens her bedroom door.)*

FUNMI. We were just having a heated debate –

*(***REY*** gets up and goes to the door.)*

REY. – About the positives and negatives of migration.

> (**ELLE** *gets up and goes to the door.*)

ELLE. – And-and whether its problems are man-made or...
God's... rapture?

> (**SHAN** *gets up and goes to the door.*)

SHAN. – And photosynthesis uncle!

> (*They all turn to* **SHAN** *with a 'what the
> fuck?' look.*)

FUNMI'S DAD. (*Offstage.*) That's good. When you are
finished, to bed please ladies. Good night and God
bless.

> (**FUNMI** *turns off the lights. They are now
> illuminated by the light from the TV.*)

ELLE. Let's just lower the volume.

FUNMI. Not too low, I like hearing the Yoruba.

ELLE. But you don't speak it.

FUNMI. I do... sometimes.

ELLE. But you're not like fluent.

FUNMI. My parents spoke it to us growing up, so I will
be fluent before I die.I want to debate with my dad in
Yoruba and win.

SHAN. I hate it when my aunties and uncles ask me if I
can speak Yoruba man and when I say no they laugh at
me. Even though I can understand it, so I know when
they're chatting shit about me. (*In a Nigerian accent.*)
***O tirin**, does sickle cell make you skinny, maybe I
should try it.*

ELLE. Shan, how you feeling today?

SHAN. Not too bad. Just fighting my fatigue a bit.

REY. Why do you always have to bring negative energy Elle?

I knew I should've bought my crystals with me.

ELLE. Why do you even have crystals?

REY. My aunty bought them for me to cleanse bad vibes, said I could use it to talk with my mum.

SHAN. How does it work?

REY. They only work on a full moon. That's when the veil between realms is thinner.

ELLE. How do you know it's your mum you're talking to and not some demon or something?

REY. She don't like you, so I know it's my mum.

ELLE. *(Mumbles.)* Her mum's never even met me.

SHAN. Does anyone ever think about what they'd do if their parents died? No offense Rey.

REY. Very offended but please continue.

ELLE. We'll be adults soon and things like this can start happening.

REY. I was two when my mum died. Death doesn't wait for you to grow up.

SHAN. I wouldn't be able to handle my sickle cell without my mum, so I'm going with her. The way she soothes me when I have a crisis. Love that woman.

FUNMI. Same. If it's my dad I'm going with him. I hate it when he jokes about him not being around. *(Imitates her dad.) When I'm gone, you and your brother and sister,* "**Iwo lo ma j'ogun mi**", *you will inherit me* – and I'm like dad don't say that. You're going to live forever, I'm sorry to tell you but your application for death has been denied.

(**SHAN** *and* **FUNMI** *high-five.*)

FUNMI. Like sometimes I wonder if my mum even likes me? Like if she wasn't my mum, I don't think we'd be friends. Cos one minute we're gisting, but then she switches and she's treating me like an inmate.

ELLE. My mum said Little Mix was a bad influence and I shouldn't be watching their music videos.

FUNMI. Yet I'm old enough to look after my younger brother, when they went to Nigeria for a month. Kept him fed, washed, took him to school and put him to bed. And did social services come and collect us?

REY. I think my dad would return me if he could but the feelings mutual. He's always on at me being out, thinking I'm having sex all the time because he doesn't understand what Queer means. He loves to project because I know my step-mum ain't giving him none.

SHAN. I would defo return my dad. I would like to speak to the manager – this dad doesn't work. I'd like an exchange please.

ELLE. You know forgiveness is the only thing that will set you both free. As followers of Christ, we are called to forgive our parents as he forgave us, freely and without limits.

SHAN. He didn't even remember it was my birthday. No card or text as usual.

REY. – Why are we even talking about him? He's as dead to Shan, as my mum is to me. In fact he's worse cos he's still breathing.

SHAN. Yeah, at least your mum wanted you.

FUNMI. Rey, you good?

REY. You just learn to live with a gap in your life, questions in your heart. All I know is my mum wanted me to live and do everything she didn't get to do.

FUNMI. I bet your mum's really proud of you, price tag princess.

SHAN. Yeah you're the bougie bitch of her dreams. Great face with great taste.

> (**ELLE** *takes* **REY***'s hand, she holds on for a moment before* **REY** *snatches her hand back.*)

REY. Why you always so moist man? Even your hand's wet.

SHAN. Do you want to finish the film now?

ELLE. Yeah before my dad arrives.

> (**FUNMI** *restarts the film. They all bunch up together except for* **REY**.)

> (**REY** *gets a notification and whips out her phone. She smiles when she opens the message and texts back.*)

FUNMI. Who you texting?

REY. No one.

SHAN. Well someone's making you smile like that.

REY. Smile like what?

FUNMI. Like how I would if Solomon proposed.

REY. It's nothing, someone just sent me a meme.

SHAN. Who is it then?

REY. I don't have to tell you who I'm texting! You don't run me.

> (**FUNMI** *and* **SHAN** *look at each other and nod.* **FUNMI** *and* **SHAN** *launch themselves at* **REY** *pinning her to the floor. One of them tries to sit on top of* **REY**.)

REY. What are you doing? Get the fuck off me!

FUNMI. Shan get her phone!

SHAN. I can't I've got her legs! Elle, grab her phone!

FUNMI. She's strong you know, Elle get it!

REY. Elle, help me!

FUNMI. Se kia. Grab the phone!

> (**ELLE** *gets the phone but doesn't know what to do with it. She has a quick nosy.*)

> (**FUNMI** *grabs the phone from* **ELLE** *and tries to read the messages whilst* **SHAN** *has to free* **REY**. **REY** *goes for* **SHAN**.)

SHAN. *(Makes prayer hands)* Sickle cell – sickle cell – sickle cell!

> (**REY** *points at* **SHAN** *first and then uses her thumb to drag it from one side of her neck to the other.*)

REY. Give me my phone!

FUNMI. *(scrolling through messages)* One sec.

> (**REY** *stands with her arm and hand extended out waiting for* **FUNMI** *to place the phone in her hand.*)

> (**SHAN** *is visibly winded. She goes to get her bottle of water. She sips from her bottle, as she discreetly takes some painkillers.*)

> (**FUNMI** *like a child in trouble, shoves the phone into* **REY**'s *hand. When* **REY** *has the phone she also grabs* **FUNMI**'s *hand and drags her down to the floor.*)

REY. You're lucky I don't slap that smirk off your face, don't ever read my messages.

FUNMI. Let go, let go, you're hurting me man...

(**REY** *lets go of* **FUNMI**'s *hand.*)

FUNMI. Who's Azure? She your girlfriend?

SHAN. Oooooh.

REY. She's not my girlfriend.

FUNMI. She's look pretty – your type.

ELLE. She looks older than us.

REY. You don't know my type. And she's not that old.

SHAN. Who is she then?

FUNMI. She coming to prom?

ELLE. But we're supposed to be going as a group.

REY. She's my mentor! Fuck's sake.

SHAN.: Why do you have a mentor?

REY. Cos I'm not basic like you bitches.

FUNMI. And why she messaging you so late, that's a bit sus?

REY. Time difference innit, she's not in the UK. She's a passport babe.

FUNMI. And she's mentoring you in...?

REY. Stuff!

ELLE. What stuff?

REY. Nunya business stuff.

ELLE. Whatever is done in the dark will always come to light?

REY. What are you on about?

ELLE. You wouldn't need to hide her if she was legit?

REY. I'm not hiding her.

ELLE. It's not safe to talk to strangers on the internet. They could be anyone. What if she suggests you meet up when she's in London or something? And before you know it, you've been trafficked to another country.

REY. You have no idea, what you're talking about.

ELLE. Did she tell you to save her number under just one name, no surname like you're her little secret or something.

REY. Secrets? You would know all about that wouldn't you?

ELLE. I'm just saying she's too old to be interested in someone as young as you.

REY. Really Elle? Is that why your mum's divorcing your dad? He find someone younger?

FUNMI. What?

SHAN. Is that true?

ELLE. I'm going to call my dad to come pick me up. I'll wait downstairs.

(**FUNMI** *and* **SHAN** *try to stop* **ELLE** *from leaving.*)

FUNMI. Don't go.

SHAN. Why didn't you tell us?

(**ELLE** *looks down and shrugs her shoulders.*)

(**SHAN** *gives* **ELLE** *a hug, and* **FUNMI** *hugs them both.*)

You should stay. We don't even have to talk about it, if you don't want to.

ELLE. I'm just going to the bathroom.

(**ELLE** *exits.*)

SHAN. Rey – what the fuck?

FUNMI. If you aired out my parents business like that, *ma fo eti e*.

REY. *(Giggles.)* I love it when you talk dirty to me.

FUNMI. I said I'd break your ear with a slap.

SHAN. You owe Elle an apology.

REY. No. She owes her parents an apology. *(Scoffs.)* She's the best they could produce?

FUNMI. You're better than this Rey.

REY. ...It's tiring.

FUNMI. We'll go downstairs, shout when you've kissed and made up.

REY. I'm not kissing that frog.

> (**ELLE** *returns.*)

> *(They all turn to* **ELLE***, trying to hide the fact that they've all been talking about her.)*

SHAN. We're going downstairs to check for ice cream.

FUNMI. Yeah. We'll bring it up shortly. Any requests? Neapolitan?

ELLE. Chocolate chip?

FUNMI. Neapolitan it is.

> (**SHAN** *and* **FUNMI** *exit.*)

> *(Awkward silence between* **REY** *and* **ELLE***.)*

REY. Elle...

ELLE. I'm leaving.

REY. Wait. Just... slow down... it wasn't my place to air your business out like that. And for that I am sorr... I apologise.

ELLE. *(Folds hands.)* And I hope you can find space in your heart to forgive me too.

REY. Oh my days, you're so holier than thou, it's like you're trying to one-up Mother Theresa.

(**ELLE** *goes in for a hug, and* **REY** *lets her.*)

But I do mean everything else I've ever said about you though

(Beat.)

How are you doing?

ELLE. I don't want to talk about it or I'll end up crying again.

REY. You'll get through this. You're Elle nothing ever gets to you.

(Soft knocks on the door.)

(**SHAN** *and* **FUNMI** *return with bowls and a tub of ice cream.*)

SHAN. Aloha? We come in treats.

FUNMI. Take it my hands are freezing.

(They hand out bowls and spoons, they sit around the tub of ice cream. **FUNMI** *opens it.*)

ELLE. Why's it red? What flavour is that?

FUNMI. Ahh mum man. We usually take the labels off when it's not ice cream.

REY. Is it stew?

FUNMI. Nah it's period blood – course it's stew!

SHAN. I'll put it back in the freezer.

FUNMI. Leave it. I was meant to take it out to defrost anyway.

(**REY** *goes back to texting.*)

If Rey's got a date, then I'm getting a date.

(**REY** *ignores them and continues texting.*)

ELLE. No. Stick to the plan. We'll have more fun together, right Shan?

SHAN. Yeah.

FUNMI. Plan A's dead, I'm executing plan B.

ELLE. The plan isn't dead. It has risen.

SHAN. What's Plan B?

FUNMI. Going to Morrison boys' next football match, gonna reactivate my LinkedIn profile, never know, might snag an entrepreneur, you know someone on my level.

(**FUNMI** *goes to get a book that she has hidden in her room.*)

And I nicked this book of Yoruba proverbs from the library, going to use them as incantations.

SHAN. Why you stealing books from the library?

FUNMI. Reparations innit, 'cause why am I speaking English? I should be speaking Yoruba and stealing an English book.

ELLE. You don't need this.

FUNMI. You can use proverbs to pray, as blessings and charms. Some love charms ask for blood but it doesn't have to be human.

ELLE. Whose blood does it have to be then?

FUNMI. Animals?

ELLE. You can't kill an animal for prom!

SHAN. You're not going to do that are you Funmi?

FUNMI. Nah, I was just gonna go to the butcher's I only need a little bit anyway.

ELLE. Don't go down this route, you don't know what you could be getting yourself into. You're a Christian and the only blood we should be consuming is Christ's.

FUNMI. Yoruba isn't just a language it has its own religion. So keep your *funfun* beliefs to yourself.

> (**FUNMI** *waves the book over* **ELLE**'s *head and she freaks out, which makes everyone burst out laughing.*)

ELLE. *(Clutching her crucifix necklace.)* Hail Mary, full of grace, the Lord is with thee; blessed art thou amongst women, and blessed is the fruit of thy womb, Jesus.

FUNMI. Ah – ah we all worship the same god.

ELLE. Don't do this – think of your soul!

SHAN. Rey-Rey-Rey!

FUNMI. Can you stop texting your bae for like one second?

REY. Maybe if you had a mentor then you'd understand. Not having a date for prom is not the end of the world – it's just the end of this chapter – there are still more chapters to come.

> (**REY**'s *phone buzzes.*)

Don't wait for me, finish the film.

> (**REY** *exits to take a call.*)

REY. *(on her phone)* Hey Azure.

FUNMI. (to **SHAN** & **ELLE**) What the fuck?

ELLE. Rey's got a point – prom is just one night for us. We don't need anyone else to celebrate it.

> (*The sound of a car honking its horn outside.*)

ELLE. My dad's here. O dabo forever.

SHAN & FUMI. O dabo forever.

(**ELLE** *exits.*)

FUNMI. Why would she think I wouldn't understand?

SHAN. I'm sure she didn't mean it like that. There's less than four months of school left. It's gonna go so quick. Prom is gonna be great because of the memories we make.

FUNMI. Whatever! I still want to wine on somebody's son.

SHAN. You can wine on me – I'll catch it!

(**FUNMI** *and* **SHAN** *each pick up a pillow and simulate caching a wine. Their attempts dissolve into giggles.*)

Scene Three

(Rey's bedroom. July 2017.)

(They are getting ready for prom.)

SHAN. Elle, let's do your make-up!

ELLE. My mum said Jesus gave us natural make-up, sweat and spit.

FUNMI. **Jesu**.

REY. Your same mum with tattooed eyebrows? That's hypocritical.

      *(***FUNMI** *and* **SHAN** *chuckle.)*

ELLE. That's my mum you're talking about. She just doesn't want me to look like a temptress. Lips shouldn't be too shiny.

Do I look boring?

FUNMI. Nah but you remind me of X.

ELLE. What?

FUNMI. Find the value of X in those math equations. But really X needs to look into a mirror and say, I am beautiful, I am loved –

REY. – I do not find my worth in others.

FUNMI. No one can define me Xcept me.

      *(***REY** *and* **FUNMI** *high-five.)*

SHAN. I got predicted eight for my Art portfolio which is basically an A.

REY. Show-off.

SHAN. You'd look so good with a lip liner and some gloss on top, tiny bit of blush and I'll use the eyelash curler, not too bait just to make your natural beauty pop. We'll take it off before you go home – your mum will never know.

ELLE. But she will?

REY. How? Unless you tell her – so don't tell her.

SHAN. Elle you are so pretty. I just want you to feel it, you know, even if it's just for one night. You deserve nights like this.

FUNMI. It's okay you don't have edges –

REY. Yeah, your hair distracts from your ears.

> (**ELLE** *touches her ears, nods and* **SHAN** *excitedly does her make-up.*)

SHAN. Also, guess who's got a date for prom?

FUNMI. What? You snake!

REY. I thought we were going together. Hashtag feminist tings.

SHAN. I know but that was until Marcus Knight asked me to be his date.

REY. MK asked you?

SHAN. Don't sound so surprised.

> (**FUNMI** *gets out a notebook of names and her calculator and runs the numbers.*)

FUNMI. He's the sixth pengest boy in Morrison Boys.

ELLE. That's pretty high on the list.

SHAN. He moved up six places, after he got his ear pierced and sorted out his BO.

REY. Top ten is decent, still!

SHAN. I know right.

FUNMI. You're barely even in school! When did he ask you?

SHAN. He told me to meet him outside the library last week. My heart was racing.

REY. And you did?

FUNMI. You know that's where girls go to get fingered.

ELLE. That's why the books smell funny and the pages are always discoloured.

SHAN. I'm not stupid. I made him keep his hands in his pockets. He was so nervous I thought he was going to propose. He told me he's liked me for the longest and as school was coming to an end, he said he actually felt sad thinking that he might never see me again.

ELLE. Woah, that's so romantic.

SHAN. I've never felt like this about anyone before.

REY. What since last week?

(**REY** *retches.*)

SHAN. Like it all happened so quick. What if he is the one?

ELLE. Then you have been divinely blessed. That kind of love is rare.

FUNMI. Love?!?! You barely even know him.

SHAN. MK's on his school basketball team. He has a younger sister in year seven. And he has a four-pack. I felt it through his shirt when we hugged. I mean we might end up being that couple that fall in love in secondary school and be together for like forty years or something.

ELLE. Aww high school sweethearts.

FUNMI. You wanted to be the only one with a date. Don't think I don't know your games. I play them too.

SHAN. I don't know what you mean! We can still *go* to prom as a group. Like obvs I'll be having a dance or five with MK but we'll still have fun together. Bitch about people's outfits, take lots of pictures but if it's like a slow dance then I'll be with my hubby.

(**REY** *snort-laughs – it sounds like she's choking but also farting orally.*)

(*Everyone looks at* **REY** *– still laughing.*)

REY. She called him her hubby.

SHAN. Are you done?

(**REY** *notices* **FUNMI**'s *demeanour change.*)

REY. Funmi, you okay?

FUNMI. Yes! Actually, this is good. Shan you can help me with phase three of my plan! You can get MK to introduce me to Anthony or Antoine. Then I'm gonna pluck a hair from one of them put it in a drink and drink it, then I'm gonna pluck one of my hairs put it in his drink and get him to drink it. Then I need to be the first face whoever drinks it sees. And he'll fall in love with me instantly.

REY. My God, you don't need a date for prom. You've got me and those two weirdos over there.

FUNMI. But I want a kiss, I want someone to kiss me.

REY. I'll kiss you then, kissing ain't even all that.

FUNMI. NO! I don't want your pity kiss. I want a moment that lasts, I want a night that I look back on and think I wasn't a nobody at school, that someone saw me.

REY. But who says you have to find all that at prom? This is the beginning. When we go to college we don't wear uniforms anymore – that tells the world we are becoming adults. The world opens up for us. We get to do more, see more, be more. Stop thinking so small about some likkle party to celebrate the fact that the teachers never have to see us again. We're moving closer to becoming our real selves, fulfilling our potential. We get to set the agenda now.

FUNMI. I don't wanna hear all that. I just want to hear you say that I'm buff and that any boy would be lucky to have me.

REY. *(In a bad Nigerian accent.)* You're my sweet potato, my ripe plantain – the Supermalt to my suya. Ain't no one on this planet like you.

SHAN. All done?

> (**SHAN** *hands* **ELLE** *the lip gloss to keep.* **ELLE** *pockets the lip gloss.)*

REY. Shan you are a real artiste.

SHAN. Thanks. Do you like it Elle?

ELLE. It's still my face but like posher.

FUNMI. Where do you get the audacity?

REY. Who's that pengting with the sexy eyelashes?

FUNMI. I need her digits like yesterday.

> (**ELLE** *can't help but chuckle at all the hyping her up.)*

SHAN. We ready?

REY. *(Snaps fingers.)* **Omo**, you wish you could be buried, looking this good.

FUNMI. **Mo fine gan**.

> *(Music plays – a song the characters all enjoy like a song in the style of* **[NADIA ROSE – "SKWOD"]**. *Each one of them struts into prom wearing sunglasses. They revel in it. Maybe one of them is a little unstable in her too-high heels but it doesn't matter they all feel like supermodels.)*

Scene Four

(We see a moment of them taking in prom, the decor and music's underwhelming but they won't let that ruin the night for them.)

(They take group photos together and perform their choreographed dance.)

*(**FUNMI** and **SHAN** depart leaving **REY** and **ELLE** together.)*

*(**FUNMI** gets two drinks and her tweezers out.)*

*(**SHAN** approaches a member of the audience, they become a stand-in for Marcus. They flirt and they dance.)*

*(**FUNMI** carries two cups, she offers a cup to an audience member, hopefully no one accepts it. Then we see **FUNMI** trying to get **SHAN**'s attention, but **SHAN** has her back to her.)*

*(**FUNMI** stands alone in the centre, holding the two cups. She nods and waves as other students pass by. **FUNMI** drifts off into a dark corner.)*

*(**REY** and **ELLE** get drinks and clink their cups together before drinking.)*

*(**REY** is freer when she dances, **ELLE** stands on the sidelines watching. **REY** drags **ELLE** to the centre to dance. **REY** dances around a clapping **ELLE**. The music changes, and **REY** goes to leave the dance floor, but **ELLE** stops her, she recognises the music as a song she likes.)*

(They dance together, it's awkward. **ELLE** *accidentally gets an eyelash in her eye.* **REY** *blows too hard into* **ELLE**'s *eye and ends up temporarily blinding* **ELLE**, *who backs into a corner. When* **REY** *tries to check* **ELLE**'s *eye,* **ELLE** *leans in and kisses* **REY**, *who quickly backs away from* **ELLE**. **REY** *is stunned.)*

*(***ELLE*** *runs out, and* **REY** *checks to see if there were any witnesses before scurrying away.)*

Scene Five

(Rey's bedroom. July 2017.)

(**SHAN** *and* **FUNMI** *get ready for bed.*)

SHAN. *(Scrolling through her phone.)* I wish we took more pictures man, I don't want to forget this night, hashtag nopain, I'm not even that tired man.

FUNMI. I can't wait to get dementia so I can forget this night forever.

SHAN. God forbid.

FUNMI. So you can hear me? Here's me thinking all night I'd turned invisible. I was trying to get your attention to help me with my plan. Neither Antoine or Anthony would accept a drink from me. It was so embarrassing.

SHAN. Oh sorry, I didn't hear you - I was distracted.

FUNMI. Distracted? Are you mad? After everything Shan.

SHAN. I couldn't hear you.

FUNMI. Helping you with your coursework, sharing my notes, all the hospital visits.

SHAN. Oh, sorry I didn't realise we were racking up favours with each other.

FUNMI. You couldn't do this one thing for me.

SHAN. I said I didn't hear you. What - you want a refund?

FUNMI. Yeah... I want my family's blood back.

SHAN. What?

FUNMI. I said I want my family's blood back.

SHAN. I don't fucking have it, that's not how blood donation works.

(**FUNMI** *and* **SHAN** *stand-off, each believing they're in the right.*)

(**REY** *enters with her arms full of snacks.*)

FUNMI. You're so selfish.

SHAN. You're so selfish.

FUNMI. And ungrateful, and spoilt –

SHAN. – Spoilt?! Your dad's –

FUNMI. – What about my dad?

SHAN. You're lucky I respect him too much.

(**REY** *dumps the snacks she was holding, goes up to both of them and grabs them by the ear and brings them together.*)

SHAN & FUNMI. Ow ow ow / ow ow ow, let go.

REY. You – say sorry.

SHAN. *(Mumbles.)* Sorry.

REY. Now you – say sorry.

FUNMI. You think you're the first person to twist my ear? Finish what you have started **joh**!

(**REY** *begins dramatically twisting* **FUNMI***'s ear.*)

FUNMI. *E joo, e joo, e joo.* Sorry, Shanice.

(**REY** *lets them go,* **SHAN** *and* **FUNMI** *gasp in relief.*)

SHAN. What the fuck Rey? You know I've got sensitive ears.

REY. ...Anyone heard from Elle?

SHAN. Something happened at prom tonight –

FUNMI. – Not for me, it didn't...

SHAN. Marcus asked me to be his girlfriend!

> (**REY** *is momentarily relieved.* **FUNMI** *claps
> sarcastically.*)

– Yeahhh, that's why I was distracted. But I told him
we need to take it slow. Not had a boyfriend before and
I don't want to rush it. Like let me do some research
first.

FUNMI. Research what?!

SHAN. Rey! You've been booed up before.

REY. Look the only advice I give straight girls who date
boys is never pay for anything. Until society addresses
the gender pay gap, make him pay.

> (**SHAN** *and* **FUNMI** *groan and roll their eyes.*)

FUNMI. Okay Audre Lorde, now is not the time. Shan,
does Marcus know about your blood sucking?

SHAN. Nah, it doesn't matter.

FUNMI. If Marcus truly likes you then he'll like everything
that comes with you.

SHAN. And he does!

FUNMI. But what about when you have your next crisis?

SHAN. Get off my back, you're starting to sound jealous.

FUNMI. Jealous. Jealous? Jell-us?

REY. *(Interjects.)* Elle kissed me tonight?

SHAN. What?!

FUNMI. *(Throws her hands up.)* I'm going to die alone.
Cool.

SHAN. Gabrielle?

FUNMI. As in Angel Gabrielle?

SHAN. Saint Gabrielle of St. Josephine's Girl's School?

REY. Yep, she licked me down on the dance floor.

SHAN & FUNMI. *Ko* possible. / Nahhh.

REY. Why would I lie?

SHAN. Are you sure she wasn't drinking?

REY. – You can't get drunk off Shloer.

SHAN. But it's made from grapes and wine is made from grapes.

REY. – It's a non-alcoholic drink. It literally says it on the bottle.

FUNMI. You can't always trust what's on the packaging. Remember that horse meat scandal.

REY. Elle wasn't drunk. She was filled with something but it wasn't alcohol.

SHAN. Do you like Elle like that?

REY. Do you want me to slap you?

FUNMI. Maybe she was trying to baptise you with her lips. I'm just trying to get into Elle's mind.

REY. How would you feel if I just walked up to you and kissed you with no warning? We've all been friends since year seven. I thought she would have said something.

SHAN. So does that mean she's a lesbian?

REY. Didn't get a chance to debrief, did I? She ran off.

FUNMI. Maybe she isn't. Like maybe because she knows you, she felt she could, I don't know, just try it.

REY. I saw the panic in her eyes. She is, even if she's not ready to admit it. Trying to hide it can really fuck up your mind.

FUNMI. My parents are strict, but Elle's mum. Boy...

SHAN. I'll just send her a voice note asking if she's alright. And if she's a lesbian?

REY. No you won't! That's her business, mind your own.

FUNMI. Leave her. I'll drop her a message, but I won't make it bait.

Scene Six

(We are inside their phones. July–August 2017.)

SHAN. Happy Birthday Rey! Welcome to the sixteen club! Finally!

Wishing you a bless up year! Love you long time bitch!

REY. I own the club.

Thanks babe.

You coming Pxssy Palace with us?

SHAN. Hospital said I have stay a little longer

I thought I'd be out by now

Crying face emoji

REY. Middle finger emoji – to your sickle cell

Get well soon Dracula

SHAN. Middle finger emoji.

FUNMI. Happy Birthday, Leo Princess!

First of her name, Queen of the Rebellion.

And breaker of bludclart bank accounts!

REY. You coming Pxssy Palace, Funmi?

Azure's coming and I told her all about you

FUNMI. Don't know emoji

My baby face will give us away.

REY. I'll do your make-up, so you don't look like a cherub.

FUNMI. Fine but I'll have to be back home before midnight.

REY. Midnight?!?!?!

Angry face emoji

FUNMI. Take it or leave it?

REY. God, didn't know I was friends with such.

Grandma emoji.

FUNMI. You coming @Elle??

> *(There is no response from* **ELLE.***)*

***

SHANI. @Elle Hellooooo?

Just checking you're alive.

> *(***ELLE** *reads the message but doesn't reply.)*

Okay two ticks will have to do then.

Where have you been hiding?

You going to ignore me?

I'm not going to stop

Sending you messages.

Miss you.

Why wont you reply?

Where are you?

You at least coming results day?

Doctors think I'll be out by then.

ELLE. *(Hesitates.)* Thumbs up emoji.

SHAN. Good.

We're all worried about you.

Funmi went to your house.

And your dad said that you were away.

Hope your having fun wherever you are?

***

(**REY**, **SHAN** *and* **FUNMI** *each step into a spotlight. They bring out envelopes. They each catch their breath before opening their envelopes.* **FUNMI** *is relieved,* **REY** *folds the paper and puts it in her pocket.* **SHAN** *scrunches up the paper into a ball and throws it in a bin.* **SHAN** *gets a text message, she opens it and gets upset.)*

Scene Seven

(Shan's bedroom. August 2017.)

*(**SHAN** and **FUNMI** are sat on Shan's bed as she wipes away tears. **REY** is performing a cleansing ceremony with her crystals.)*

SHAN. I was a girlfriend for five weeks... and four days...

REY. Your relationship was barely a foetus –

FUNMI. – What Rey is trying to say is MK doesn't deserve your tears. They're too precious to be wasted on him.

SHAN. When was the last time you've been dumped?

REY. I am a dumper never been a dumpee.

FUNMI. So what happened?

SHAN. He texted me, this morning after he got his results...

*(**REY** and **FUNMI** gasp.)*

REY. Son of bitch.

FUNMI. Seed of a bastard.

SHAN. *(Nods.)* Said it'll be worse if he did it in person. His auntie died of sickle cell years ago. It'll fuck up his studies if anything happens to me and he's on track to get into Oxford. He said we can still be friends but I couldn't read the rest... what if he's right, what if I don't have a future?

FUNMI. You can't punish yourself for something you have no control over.

SHAN. I don't have to, the world is punishing me on a daily.

FUNMI. Sometimes we have to keep fighting –

SHAN. – But what am I fighting for?

FUNMI. If you let me finish – Sometimes we have to keep fighting even if we're not sure if we'll win.

SHAN. But I'm tired all the time. Don't you get bored of me? We missed Comic Con and Love Box.

REY. Bitch if I'm bored – I'll let you know.

FUNMI. As long as Solomon still lives under this roof, I'm always going to find a reason to swing by.

*(**SHAN** chuckles.)*

REY. *(Whips out phone.)* So what does everyone want from Creams, my treat, to celebrate our wins and losses?

*(A knock on the bedroom door. Enter **ELLE**.)*

ELLE. Aloha!

SHAN. Elle!

*(**SHAN** leaps up to hug **ELLE**.)*

FUNMI. The prodigal son has returned

*(**FUNMI** goes to hug **ELLE**.)*.

FUNMI. Missed your sermons.

SHAN. Innit. You look different.

FUNMI. Where have you been? You didn't reply to my messages.

ELLE. I was at this Christian summer camp, it was a gift from my parents. They were quite strict about phones there; I think my parents wanted me away so they could work on their marriage.

REY. Where was it?

ELLE. Bournemouth.

SHAN. Is that near Dagenham?

FUNMI. And that's why you didn't pass Geography.

REY. You enjoy it?

ELLE. Yeah it was great. To be surrounded by nature, water and be reminded we are all God's miracles.

FUNMI. Now that we're all here. What did you get?

ELLE. Mostly sevens.

REY. Feel all superior because you got the best results.

FUNMI. No, course not. It feels fucking brilliant being the smartest person in the room. *Bow down bitches.*

REY. I got an eight in French – ***connasse***! but my dad and step-mum weren't too happy about the rest.

SHAN. I'm going to have to resit Maths and English but my mum's getting the doctors to write a letter to the college to let them know about my situation. I should be able to do my resits there, cos, I'm not spending another year at St Josephine's without you lot.

FUNMI. God forbid.

REY. What about your predicted eight in Art?

SHAN. I got a six.

FUNMI. You saying it like you failed?

SHAN. Cos I did.

REY. Shan, GCSEs are just memory tests. What are we going to do with algebra, magnetism, or river formations? Waste of time.

FUNMI. You should do business studies with me, then we'll never have to answer to anyone.

SHAN. Maybe?

REY. What is your business going to be boss lady?

FUNMI. I don't know. Maybe I could, be an art dealer and sell Shan's art. You could be the next Banksy.

REY. Shanksy!

SHAN. I won't be the next Banksy if I can't even stay well enough to pass some shit exams.

REY. School can never define you. Azure said school was designed to ignore your untapped potential. You have to learn to harness your potential and use it as fuel to reach heights you couldn't even imagine. So my dad and my step-mum said if I ace my A-Levels, they'll get me my first whip.

SHAN. Woah.

FUNMI. A whole car?

REY. Once I can get myself around, I'll be out of that house for good.

(**ELLE** *looks down.*)

ELLE. I... I... I won't be going to college –

SHAN. Yes you are!

ELLE. Well I am, just not with you lot. My mum's enrolled me at this Catholic sixth form in Chis-wick. (*Pronounces it chiss-wick.*)

REY. It's Chiswick.

SHAN. Is that even in London?

(**FUNMI** *shushes* **SHAN**.)

ELLE. West London. It's a good college.

FUNMI. Do you have to wear a uniform?

ELLE. Yeah.

FUNMI. Peak!

REY. Is that where you want to go though?

ELLE. I just want to make my parents proud.

FUNMI. The band is splitting up.

SHAN. We should be going out together more, making memories! We said we'd go to Southend one weekend!

ELLE. We can still do all that on the weekends, and we can do video calls and do study sessions.

SHAN. First MK dumps me and now Elle's not coming with us.

ELLE. I'm sorry about MK Shan, I saw the messages –

REY. Oh! So your phone does work?

> (**FUNMI** *makes a warning sound and shakes her head to not bring up drama.*)

FUNMI. What did you want from Creams? Red Velvet cake Rey? / Elle what do you want?

ELLE. / If you've got something to say to me then say it.

FUNMI. Cool, I'll surprise you then.

REY. I know this gal ain't trying to step to me.

FUNMI. Shan let's go order everyone desserts out there.

SHAN. Girl it's just getting good.

REY. The same girl who at prom - You remember prom right? Shan did your make-up, Funmi was on a juju mission and you wiggled your slimy lips on mine?

ELLE. No I didn't.

FUNMI. Shan I'm gonna need you to read between the lines, like you didn't in your English exam.

SHAN. Too soon.

FUNMI. (*Snaps her fingers.*) ***Bo si bi***

> (**SHAN** *and* **FUNMI** *exit.*)

*(Tension in the air between **REY** and **ELLE**. **ELLE** starts scrolling on her phone to distract herself.)*

REY. You attacked me with your lips.

ELLE. I didn't attack – look okay I'm sorry. I wasn't myself. I promise it will never happen again. I should have said it sooner.

REY. You can't just go around kissing people!

ELLE. Can we put this behind us? I still want to be your friend.

REY. Well friends have to be honest with each other.

ELLE. You're right.

REY. How long have you known that you're not into boys?

ELLE. I'm not. I mean, I am.

REY. It's not me you need to convince.

ELLE. I do like boys.

REY. ...And girls too. Look being bisexual is not that big of a deal –

ELLE. – I'm not that. I just care about people a lot and sometimes I get confused about how to show that. The camp helped me learn to self correct. You won't be seeing that behaviour from me ever again.

REY. What did you do at this camp?

ELLE. We had Bible study, a bonfire and prayed together.

REY. Ahh. I think I know the camp you went to, heard someone mention it before. Bournemouth right? What was the name of it again?

ELLE. ... I've actually forgotten it. LOL.

REY. You forgot the name of the camp you were at all summer? Funny that… you know they give out leaflets at Black Pride telling you how to report those 'camps'.

ELLE. It was a present from my parents. A trip away and I'm grateful for it.

(**REY** *sees* **ELLE** *is shaking and tries to put an arm around her. But* **ELLE** *shoves* **REY** *hard.*)

REY. OWWW! What the fuck!

ELLE. Sorry, sorry, sorry.

(**ELLE** *tries to help* **REY** *up, but she refuses and gets up on her own.* **ELLE** *pinches herself several times.*)

I didn't mean to.

REY. You know you can talk to me, when you're not shoving me or trying to kiss me.

(**ELLE** *clenches her fists.*)

ELLE. I went home after prom and told my mum what happened, they said I should tell them any time I get those feelings. They told me to pack a bag, and drove to Bournemouth, to this pastor's house. There were other people my age there. The pastor asked me all these… questions. He told me how evil… people… like that were and that if I wanted to join in on their evil ways then I couldn't call myself a Christian.

REY. What the fuck! Evil?

ELLE. They gave me a special soap to bath with… it stung my skin and I had to drink these things that they said would flush the sin out of me… and we had these night vigils but I understand now. It's strengthened my relationship with God. I am a Christian and that's not how Christians behave.

REY. Well you're obviously not straight Elle. Even God could tell you that. I know you're scared and it can seem like a lot. But you can be a happy, queer, black woman.

ELLE. I can't live like you do, it's not the same for me..

REY. What's that supposed to mean?

ELLE. You don't know what it's like to grow up with Black Christian parents.

You get to do what you want, say what you want, be what you want.

REY. Oh don't give me that bullshit.

ELLE. But you were raised by your white dad and white step-mum.

REY. Like that was a choice? For someone with your grades, you're being really dumb right now.

ELLE. It's a sin. It's not what black people do. It's not of our nature. It's un-African.

REY. Can you hear yourself? Do you really believe that?

ELLE. I have to. I can do all things through Christ, who strengthens me.

REY. I've never felt sadder for you Elle. I can see how brainwashed you are. / If you truly believe you deserve to be punished, who am I to say otherwise. But the fact that we're standing here now, is because we are descendants of Queer survivors. We're not the first and we won't be the last.

ELLE. / "Be on guard. Stand firm in the faith. Be courageous. Be strong."

(**REY** *exits as* **ELLE** *repeats the Bible quote.*)

Scene Eight

(Funmi's bedroom. March 2018.)

*(**FUNMI** walks into her bedroom. There is a hole in the middle of her room. It lights up and dims like the rhythm of a heartbeat. **FUNMI** edges slowly closer to it as the light begins to dim out. When she goes to reach inside the hole, she is interrupted by –)*

(A knock on her door.)

*(Enter **SHAN**, dressed in a traditional skirt and blouse tailored attire with a modern twist.)*

*(**FUNMI** looks up and takes in **SHAN**'s outfit. **FUNMI** slow-claps.)*

*(**SHAN** rushes to hug an unreceptive **FUNMI**. **SHAN** hugs her for a long while.)*

*(**SHAN** picks up an empty glass bottle from the dresser.)*

SHAN. Not you sipping on the Jesus juice.

FUNMI. It's Shloer. Rey was right, it can't get you drunk.

SHAN. You look good, can I say that? Honestly you do, your skin's glowing, you're looking extra thick in all the right places –

FUNMI. – Shan, my dad's died, I've not had a BBL. These compliments, *oti poju*, it's too much fam.

SHAN. Sorry, I just… I don't know what to say.

FUNMI. You don't have to say anything.

(They sit in a heavy silence.)

(**SHAN** *opens her water bottle and takes a few sips.* **SHAN** *slips a tablet into her mouth and then drinks some more water.*)

(*They look around the room before making eye contact at each other. They smile then look away.*)

(**ELLE** *softly knocks on the door.*)

(**ELLE** *wears a hoodie over her traditional attire in a different style made from the same fabric as* **SHAN** *and* **FUNMI**.)

ELLE. Can I come in?

SHAN. Is Rey with you?

ELLE. Nah.

SHAN. Okay, I'll message her.

(**ELLE** *gives* **FUNMI** *the biggest squeeze.*)

FUNMI. Elle… Elle… A little tight.

ELLE. *(Getting upset.)* Sorry… sorry. *(Wipes her face and clears her throat.)* How's your mum and the rest of the fam?

FUNMI. My brother won't stop calling my dad's phone to hear his voice. And my sister, I don't know where she went, probably gone to be with her not-so-secret boyfriend. Mum's panicking a bit, turns out it's expensive to die on the weekend. My dad's family in Nigeria are talking about, they want him buried over there and my mum's like but who's gon' pay for that?

ELLE. Your poor mum, sounds like she has a lot on her plate.

SHAN. Is there anything we can do? I don't know much about funerals.

FUNMI. People die. You bury them. It's natural innit.

My dad says, when he dies he'll haunt me and my siblings gently. I told him to leave money everywhere so I'll know it's him. If you find any, it's mine.

SHAN. I believe you will see him again, ain't that right resident pastor?

ELLE. Says it in the Bible.

SHAN. So how did he die?

FUNMI. I don't know what caused it. It's not like he was sick, or on any medication or anything.

>   *(Beat.)*

Obviously I was getting ready for our link up to see *Black Panther*, when my mum came in and asked me to take a seat. *(Tries not to laugh)* And I'm thinking can you not see that I'm already sat down trying to do my eyeliner. Then she said dad's colleagues found him...

ELLE. May he rest in paradise.

FUNMI. I was really looking forward to this since seeing the trailer and we haven't linked up in a while but by the time I got to my door I realised I couldn't come. Is that bad? That I really wanted to come anyway...

>   *(An alarm goes off on **FUNMI***'s phone.)*

The film starts in an hour, you can still make it if you leave now. I heard Letitia Wright was going to drop by.

SHAN. Don't be silly, we're not going anywhere. Wakanda can wait. *(Crosses her arms, doing the Wakanda Forever salute.)* Fortunata fruits forever!

ELLE. Fortunata fruits forever!

>   *(They get a notification from their group chat.)*

SHAN. It's from Rey. She says she's at a surprise retreat with Azure that she can't get out of. She's ditched us again!

FUNMI. I'm starting to hate that mentor. What kind of name is Azure anyway?

SHAN. And for a black woman!

FUNMI. I haven't been seeing her at college.

ELLE. Rey sent another message. She says: *(Earnestly reading message.)* "Funmi, I won't lie to you, it's going to get worse before it gets better, and then it's gonna get even more worse, then it might get a little better and you think you've finished before it gets worser..."?

FUNMI. Bun that negative energy. Return to sender. What's poppin' in Shanland?

SHAN. So I'm seeing this new guy Malachi. We met at McDonald's. He works there and he gave me a free McFlurry.

FUNMI. Couldn't give you a free burger? Cheapskate.

SHAN. I like him, and he knows about my sickle cell. His nan has dementia so he's used to being around sick people.

ELLE. How long has it been?

SHAN. We just celebrated our three-month anniversary, I've not had a crisis since we met. He told me I was the type of girl he'd been looking for even though he doesn't usually date brunettes. He even said he wants to introduce me to his family.

> (**FUNMI** *takes* **SHAN**'s *hands in hers.* **FUNMI** *strokes* **SHAN**'s *face lovingly.*)

FUNMI. Babes, I don't know which Caucasian lied to you – you're not a brunette.

SHAN. What you on about? Yes I am and so are you both.

ELLE. Dua Lipa is a brunette but Normani isn't.

FUNMI. See even our resident monk over there knows.

SHAN. What would you call Beyoncé then?

> (**FUNMI** *and* **ELLE** *shake their heads.*)

FUNMI. Let's put it this way Meg Thee Stallion... Cardi... Doja... Nicki... Lizzo... are not, and will never be, brunettes.

ELLE. But Ariana Grande, Demi Lovato, Harry Styles, Jade from Little Mix are brunettes.

FUNMI. However Leigh-Anne from Little Mix isn't, *sho* get?

SHAN. So what are we then?

FUNMI. Black. We can rock any hair colour but we're always going to be black.

ELLE. Show us a picture of him then?

> (**SHAN** *gets out her phone and begins scrolling through a lot of photos.*)

FUNMI. Seems like a lot of photos.

SHAN. Just trying to find one with good lighting.

FUNMI. So this where you go when you're off sick yeah?

SHAN. Nah I'm home... mostly.

ELLE. I hope you've been looking after yourself.

> (**SHAN** *reveals a picture of him on her phone to them.*)
>
> (*Awkward pause.*)

FUNMI. Why you showing us a stock photo?

> (**SHAN** *looks at her phone to check.*)

SHAN. That's Malachi.

FUNMI. *E gba mi o*. This boy is white.

SHAN. And...?

FUNMI. But you said his name was Malachi.

SHAN. There are white people called Malachi. It's in the Bible, isn't it Elle?

ELLE. *(Not confidently.)* I don't know, I'm not the Bible.

FUNMI. You know white boys. He can kill you, chop you up and feed you to his dog. Do you want to become a documentary?

SHAN. He doesn't have a dog – he's got a cat.

FUNMI. So you want to become cat food?

SHAN. Don't start with all that, you should only date black boys –

FUNMI. – White boys grow up into white men.

SHAN. Who don't get sickle cell or pass on the trait.

FUNMI. Are you dating my man for his blood?

ELLE. I don't think dating someone because of their blood type is healthy.

SHAN. I'm not a vampire. My life isn't a joke. I have to think about my future every day – whether I'll have kids or not, when do I check if my boyfriend has the trait, do I get him to do a blood test on the first date? Will I even live long enough to start a family? This drove my dad away, it scared off Marcus –

FUNMI. – You will live long.

SHAN. You don't know that. Every crisis is just that. A crisis - because I don't know if I will survive it. I can be in so much pain my body just shuts down, I pass out and I don't know if I'll wake up. Like I don't feel safe when I'm alone, what it if I can't reach my phone in time or I can't get to A&E in time, is this it for me?

(*Beat.*)

FUNMI. I didn't know that's how bad it gets.

SHAN. There's always this assumption that you'll see me again. It's hard not to feel like I'm running out of time.

(**ELLE** *rubs* **SHAN**'s *back softly.*)

ELLE. You're here now, that's all that matters.

FUNMI. When I think of my mum and dad, they are like the sky and the sea. They're both their own elements, and science tells us they could never meet, but if you look beyond the horizon they pour into each other. When my mum hears my dad come home from work, I see her body relax. When they speak to each other it's like a chemical reaction – they radiate it, you feel it. He mellows her out and she gathers him up. And it's like I can feel that here with you guys.

ELLE. Me too...

FUNMI. It's like I can still feel him here. Whispering. Trying to keep me close to my culture, but in a way that makes me feel proud. Still listening to me, really trying to understand me.

(**ELLE** *is visibly upset.*)

ELLE. I wish my mum was like your dad. I won't ever be good enough for her.

SHAN. What do you mean?

ELLE. I've tried everything. I get the grades, I don't stay out late, I don't chat back, I go to church, I go to Bible study, I eat what she wants, dress how she wants me to, think how she wants me to and it still isn't... she threatened to send me to Jamaica, to go live with some sister.

SHAN. She's just saying that.

FUNMI. Yeah my mum says that to me all the time. *(As her mum.)* You think life is hard yeah, just wait to till you reach Lagos. No electricity, no running water and lots of lizards, then you will learn to listen.

ELLE. My mum doesn't make threats she doesn't follow through on.

FUNMI. Did you lot argue or something?

ELLE. This college she made me go to, it makes all the students her bitch. They give us so much work we're doing 5 A-Levels because RE is compulsory.

FUNMI. Shit!

ELLE. I'm tired. I'm studying all the time, I haven't even really made any friends there. But this one time in sociology, I literally couldn't stay awake, by the time the class ended I had no notes. This girl must have seen and shared her notes with me. She was cool. We started having lunch together, and doing study sessions ...then she tried to kiss me.

SHAN. Elle's got a girlfriend yeah?

ELLE. No. And I told her no. I'm not like that. Nothing happened. I told my mum that I stopped it, thinking she'd be proud but instead she said it was my fault. I must have done something that led the girl to think I was into her. She said – I disappointed her. Why couldn't I just be normal. I-I told her the truth. Like she always wants me to. But look at where the truth got me.

FUNMI. But what's your truth Elle?

ELLE. ...I might not... only like boys.

(**FUNMI** *fake gasps.*)

I know Rey already told you.

FUNMI. And it doesn't change how we feel about you.

SHAN. You're still Elle to us.

(**SHAN** *and* **FUNMI** *embrace* **ELLE**.)

ELLE. I said some things I shouldn't have said to Rey, but she was right. My mum got right in my face and said, "*I will never accept my daughter living under my roof partaking in that demonic lifestyle*". I told her "*Maybe I'm not your daughter then*". She tried to slap me but I dodged it and ran out to see you guys.

FUNMI. **Jesu Christi**. You can't go home. It's not safe there.

SHAN. You're always welcome at mine, as long as you need.

ELLE. Thanks. A part of me is scared but there is a part of me that is also relieved, because now I don't have to lie to my parents or myself anymore. I need to be living honestly.

FUNMI. You've never sounded more like yourself.

Scene Nine

(Between March 2018 and December 2018.)

(The stage splits into four bedrooms. **SHAN**, **FUNMI**, **REY** *and* **ELLE** *each stand for a moment in their respective bedrooms. They take a breath in before their year begins to race at speed. The following snapshots can happen like dominoes where one sets off the next or simultaneously.)*

*(***REY*** *picks up her phone and dials. She hangs up and redials. She keeps doing this until she gets through.)*

*(***ELLE*** *looks at her room one last time before turning off the light with her backpack and luggage.)*

*(***SHAN*** *falls asleep whilst trying to study but is awoken by a knock on her door.* **ELLE** *arrives with her backpack and luggage.* **SHAN** *hugs her and takes a bag from* **ELLE***, to get her settled in.)*

*(**Time passes.**)*

*(***REY*** *is fuming when she finally gets through to her mentor.)*

REY. *(On her phone.)* You did me dirty... after everything... If I catch your cheap-ass weave again in these streets, it's on sight. Yeah it is a threat. *Omo ale*.

*(**Time passes.**)*

*(***SHAN*** *is sat on the edge of her bed with* **ELLE**. **SHAN** *takes a deep breath in whilst* **ELLE** *rubs her shoulder comfortingly.* **SHAN** *dials a number on her phone and puts it on speaker.)*

RECORDED VOICE. *(speaker phone)* This number has not been recognised. Please hang up and try again.

SHAN. See? I told you.

(*Time passes.*)

(**FUNMI** *dances as she cleans her bedroom with her headphones on. There's a knock at the door but she doesn't hear it.* **REY** *sneaks up on her.*)

FUNMI. Blood of Jesus!

(**REY** *laughs.*)

What are you doing here?

REY. I'm here to see my favourite girl.

FUNMI. What about Azonto?

REY. You mean Azure? Oh that was nothing.

FUNMI. Oh so she dumped you and you've come crawling back.

REY. She didn't dump me. We weren't together. I told you she was my mentor.

FUNMI. Whatever. What do you want?

REY. I thought I was coming to my friend's house but maybe I'm mistaken.

FUNMI. Friends don't ghost you after your dad dies.

REY. I didn't ghost you. I just had a lot on.

FUNMI. We've all had a lot on. Elle and Shan found time.

REY. I know, I know. I fucked up. Let's start again. FUNMI! Long time, sorry I was so shit at replying to your messages and that I wasn't there for you when you needed me. Like truly sorry, like if I could go back in time and slap some sense into myself sorry!

FUNMI. Okay okay, *mo ti gbo*. So where have you been?

REY. So… I dropped out of college to work with Azure. She runs this Fempire of black women entrepreneurs. I met all these incredible successful women. She was going to show me the secrets to building my own Fempire. It started with me buying her coffees, then I was paying for her Uber's and before you know it, she wanted me to invest. I told her I can't access my trust fund 'til I'm twenty-one but she convinced me to write a cheque in my dad's name.

FUNMI. Wowu. For how much?

REY. Twenty bags

FUNMI. Come again?

REY. Twenty thousand…

      (**FUNMI** *paces.*)

FUNMI. *(in a Nigerian accent)* You know you can be prosecuted for that!

REY. I know that now! Lucky my step-mum caught me in my dad's office! She promised not to tell my dad, if I promised never to do something like that again. She wasn't even that mad at me. I think I got her all wrong, you know.

FUNMI. What nonsense Rey! 419 – at your age?!

      (**FUNMI** *dips her fingers in a glass of water and flicks it in* **REY**'s *face several times.*)

I bind and cast out any spirit of deception used against your life. / Any rituals performed in your name return to sender. In **Olodumare's** name we have prayed. **Ase.**

REY. / Funmi what the fuck.

FUNMI. You've been hard on your step-mum from day dot and look how she helped clean up your mess. Boy, she ain't like my mum.

REY. I can't believe I wasn't there to welcome you to the Dead Parent Club. I got caught up in all the glitz of hashtag softlife of these amazing gorgeous black women. They're so self-assured and certain and they had achieved so much. And I just wanted to be part of it.

FUNMI. Excuse me? You were already surrounded by amazing, gorgeous black babes!

REY. I realise that now. Like, most of the time, I feel empty... like there's nothing inside me. Not even organs. And every day, when I wake up is when the emptiness is the loudest and I try to distract myself from it. But I realised it's quieter when I'm with you lot. I've wasted so much time.

FUNMI. You're the only person I wanted to talk about my dad with. You're the one who really gets it.

REY. I'm here now.

> (**FUNMI** *isn't convinced.*)
>
> (***Time passes.***)
>
> (**SHAN** *encourages* **ELLE** *to send* **REY** *a message.*)

REY. *(replying to message)* Thumbs up emoji.

> (**REY** *and* **ELLE** *meet up to reconcile.*)

ELLE. I'm so sorry.

REY. I know... me too.

> (**REY** *and* **ELLE** *hug.*)

ELLE. So Azure?

REY. Girl – don't even get me started...

> *(Time passes.)*
>
> (**SHAN** *hasn't been feeling well but is determined to go to college, she semi-collapses and is assisted by* **ELLE**. **SHAN** *insists she is fine and goes to grab her coat/backpack but then keels over.* **ELLE** *calls for an ambulance whilst comforting* **SHAN**.)

ELLE. I need an ambulance please.

> *(Image:* **FUNMI**, **REY** *and* **ELLE**, *looking worried, sat by a semi-conscious* **SHAN** *in hospital – she breathes with an oxygen mask.)*
>
> *(Time passes.)*
>
> *(Image:* **SHAN** *sits up, feeling more like herself again.)*
>
> (**FUNMI**, **REY** *and* **ELLE** *are sat by* **SHAN**'s *bed again, happier this time.)*

FUNMI. Is Malachi still coming? Was looking forward to meeting him.

SHAN. Nah, I deaded it. Saw on socials he gave me some girl a free big mac and a milkshake.

FUNMI. Thank God. Never liked his energy.

ELLE. You being discharged today?

SHAN. Hopefully, but my haematologist has to see me first.

ELLE. I'm so proud of you, you fought two illnesses and won! That's my champ!

FUNMI. You really looked death in the face and said, "I gotta put me first! I gotta put me first!"

REY. Pneumonia who? Pneumonia where? Don't know her.

SHAN. Okay guys we're not the only ones on the ward, keep it down.

ELLE. I miss our late-night chats. If you want me to come back for a few days to help you recover I can call my dad?

SHAN. NO! I mean, no don't worry about it, I've got Solomon and my mum, I'll be alright. How is it being back at home?

ELLE. It's a compromise. Dad's the referee between me and Mum. She don't talk to me or cook for me anymore. But it's all good, just need to keep going till the end of the year, then next year I'll be in uni. I'm not applying for any uni's in London.

FUNMI. I like this side of you!

ELLE. I've decided what Mum doesn't know won't hurt her and it won't get me sent to Jamaica.

REY. You've learned the most important rule. When you have parents in your business, little white lies can save black lives.

(**SHAN**'s *phone rings, she answers it.*)

SHAN. *(On the phone.)* Hello? ...who's this, sorry – Dad?

ELLE. *(Whispers.)* We'll wait outside.

(**SHAN** *gives them a thumbs up. They exit to give* **SHAN** *her privacy.*)

SHAN. *(On the phone.)* Just my friends... yeah, I'm doing better.

(*They each put on matching pyjamas and a dressing gown with a hood, they're humming a song which we soon realise is a popular song. Each of them picks up a candle, which* **REY** *lights.)*

(They continue humming and are led out to a spot in **REY***'s garden.)*

(They face each other around a hole in the ground. They blow out their candles.)

Scene Ten

*(**REY**'s back garden. 31 December 2018.)*

FUNMI. *(Reading off her phone.)* We are gathered here today under **Olodumare's** night sky. To honour this beautiful friendship and how it laced our destinies together. May it never come undone – double knot it.

*(They **ALL** snap their fingers several times.)*

ALL. Wod-wod-wod-wod-wod-wod-wod.

SHAN. *(Clutching her hot water bottle.)* Can you hurry this all up, it's so cold. I am not starting 2019 with another crisis!

FUNMI. *(Scrolling through her phone.)* You have no sense of occasion since your near-death experience. Skip that, skip that... okay this was some beautiful stuff. 2018 was a higgy hagga year of preposterous, outlandish, insurmountable events of suffering.

REY. Clusterfuck of a year.

ELLE. Garbage fire year.

SHAN. Almost ended my life year!

FUNMI. Fuck 2018!

(They all give a rude gesture to the ground.)

We welcome in a year of joy, a year of abundance, a year of overflowing double blessings.

ELLE. We're gonna make 2019 our bitch!

SHAN. Look at Elle. Amen!

FUNMI. We have created this time capsule, an offering for our future selves as we enter the New Year. May mother nature accept and protect our treasures.

SHAN. Where's the time capsule?

FUNMI. It's here.

SHAN. You mean that takeaway box?

REY. It's Tupperware. It's indestructible.

FUNMI. Shanice, will you please step forward.

ALL. *(Whisper.)* Shanice, Shanice, Shanice.

FUNMI. What are you placing in the time capsule?

SHAN. I've brought my hospital bracelet. I know it's not going to be the last one I'll get. And I know I have to resit the whole first year of college, but I'm not going to let that stress me. I hate sickle cell so so much, but I have to learn to manage it. Learn what my triggers are and that means being honest with you lot when I'm tired or starting to feel the early signs of a crisis. I'm not going to push myself to keep up with anyone anymore. I've got to learn to live at Shan pace. It's exhausting trying force things to happen, make relationships work, when life is a gift and time is precious. I have to trust that I have time.

> (**SHAN** *places the hospital bracelet in the Tupperware.*)

FUNMI. Gabrielle, will you please step forward.

ALL. *(Whisper.)* Gabrielle, Gabrielle, Gabrielle.

FUNMI. What are you going to place in the time capsule?

ELLE. I brought the lip gloss from prom that Shan gave me. Even in my hardest year, you lot still found ways to make me smile. I went to the Open Day, at the Colchester campus of the Uni of Essex. They showed us the students union and there was a notice board and on it was a poster that said LGBTQIA but the plus was a crucifix! Why have I been spending so much time punishing myself when there are Christians like me, just living their damn lives! God never turned his back on me and I won't either. We still on for Black Pride next year?

REY. Abso-fucking-lutely!

> (**REY** and **ELLE** high five.)

> (**ELLE** puts the lip gloss in the Tupperware.)

FUNMI. Alfreda will you please step forward.

> (**REY** doesn't move.)

Alfreda?

REY. I don't know who that is.

FUNMI. Fine, REY, will you please step forward. For fuck's sake.

ALL. (Whispers.) Rey, Rey, Rey.

REY. I can't believe you bitches have got me out here showing my emotions. Let's make this quick. It's a compass.

> (**REY** chucks into the Tupperware.)

SHAN. No! Take it seriously. Do your speech!

FUNMI. Yeah, Mrs Talk-a-lot. You have nothing to say now?

REY. Fine! I brought a compass because I been feeling lost for a while and I can see now how I've hurt those closest to me.

ELLE. We've got to forgive ourselves too.

REY. My dad got me this unpaid internship at some medical equipment company in Berlin, says he doesn't want no college dropout living in his house, yammin his food, doing fuck all.

SHAN & ELLE. What?

REY. I was gonna to tell you but it made me sad thinking about it. But that's what the compass is for. That no matter how far away we are or how long we don't speak, I'll always find my way back to you lot.

FUNMI. *(Pinches* **REY.***)* You better. ***K'ama jinna sira o – oju a tun'ra ri o.***

> *(Beat.)*

SHAN. Yeah what she said.

REY. Oluwafunmilayo what are you putting in the box?

ALL. *(Whispers.)* Funmi, Funmi, Funmi.

FUNMI. I brought my dad's handkerchief from his wake. It's got a little photo of him and the dates of his life on it. I miss him every day but I'm not going to stop trying to make him proud. I'm going to ace my A-Levels so I can go to uni. *(She looks to the sky.)* I've been taking Yoruba lessons because I'm finally going to Nigeria at Easter – I can't wait to meet your family. *(She looks back at her friends.)* And I'm going to cry. I'm going to cry a lot. And that's what this handkerchief is for. For the inevitable wave of tears to come.

Fortunata Fruits, this handkerchief will dab at your tears of joy, tears of pain, tears of anger, tears of laughter, tears of winning, tears of losing. All those tears are worthy of falling, so never hold them back. Good times won't last, but neither will the bad.

> *(***FUNMI*** places the handkerchief in the Tupperware. She closes it and puts the Tupperware into the soil. It lights up. Together, they cover it with soil. They hold onto each other, until they hear the sound of fireworks begin above their heads. The look up and they don't let go.)*

POST-BLACKOUT FINALE

(They transform into a quartet and lip-sync a choreographed dance to a song in the style of Gladys Knight and the Pips – **["I'VE GOT TO USE MY IMAGINATION"]**. *Feel free to pick a song of the cast's choice, let the song seep into their bodies.)*

GLOSSARY

Aloha (Hawaiian word) Can be said as a greeting or when departing from someone (also means love and fellowship).

Konnichiwa (Japanese word) good afternoon or good day

Sayonara (Japanese word) goodbye

Connasse (French word) dickhead

Yoruba

O dabo goodbye

Oloshi a swear word (a very unlucky person)

Orisirisi all sorts (variety)

Jati-jati rubbish

O tirin they are skinny/thin

Ma fo eti e I will break your ear with a slap,
or,
I'll slap you.

Se kia hurry up

Jesu Jesus

Jesu Christi Jesus Christ

Joh Means please but can also be used to indicate different tones of a phrase

Olodumare	Supreme God of Sky, Earth, Universe. Omnipotent, transcendent, unique and all knowing.
Funfun	white
Omo	child but can also be used as slang term to address a friend
Mo fine gan	a person that is very beautiful
E joo	please
Ko possible	it's not possible
Bo si bi	come over here
Oti poju	it's too much
Sho get	do you understand/follow
E gba mi o	help me (to understand)
Omo ale	bastard
Mo ti gbo	I have heard
Ase	Has a few different meanings, one being an affirmation to seal prayers/ blessings (has a similar function to "Amen").
Iwo lo ma j'ogun mi	you will inherit me/all that I have
K'ama jinna sira o	let's keep in touch
oju a tun'ra ri o	we will meet again

Lightning Source UK Ltd.
Milton Keynes UK
UKHW020614240223
417578UK00003B/4